HELLUCINATION

Stephen Biro

CONTENTS

PREFACE

Having come to the realization that religious conviction is fundamentally a symbol system bridging the personal and the spiritual, psychologist C. G. Jung predicted the occurrence of a modern-day calamity of massive significance.

He understood what most couldn't: That though Christianity dominated the spiritual realm, it was a belief system that could only take one so far. His answer was to essentially abandon religion and encourage the valiant of soul to seek what he termed "direct contact with the unconscious." This doctrine was later expounded in Joseph Campbell's ever-popular book, *The Power of Myth*.

Despite their enthusiastic proselytizing, both men were well aware that direct contact with one's unconscious could be such an overpowering experience that it could lead to madness and, even worse, to a total disregard for a higher power.

If the potential of religious conviction is to ever achieve a regeneration of spiritual power to the extent foreseen by Jung and Campbell, individuals willing to risk direct contact with their subconscious and unconscious will be called upon to provide us with a new and enduring narrative that inspires humankind with a sense of hope, leading the way to a vibrant spirituality divorced from the dusty tales of yore. We must all stop looking for others to supply answers to the world's questions. We must instead heed the call of the unconscious to follow our dreams and seek the answers for ourselves.

Introduction to Hellucination

By David Jay Brown

One of the first discoveries that the Harvard Psychedelic Research Project made in 1962 was how important "set and setting" is when conducting a psychedelic session. Coined by Timothy Leary, the terms "set and setting" refer to the psychological mind set and the physical environment that one is in during a psychedelic experience, which can greatly influence what happens.

Decades of psychedelic drug experimentation suggest that one should be encouraged to take these powerful substances in a safe, comfortable, aesthetically-pleasing and peaceful environment that supports a spiritually-transformative experience. Otherwise, the experience can be more than a bit unpleasant, and under the wrong circumstances, it can become truly hellish.

However, despite this understanding, when Timothy Leary, Richard Albert, and Ralph Metzner wrote The Psychedelic Experience--an adaptation of The Tibetan Book of the Dead--as a guide book for LSD, mescaline, and psilocybin experiences, they neglected to realize that writing descriptions that were meant to be read aloud while tripping, which included phrases about the possibility of one becoming trapped in post-death realms, where "hungry ghosts," "wrathful deities," and "blood-drinking, flesh-eating demons" roamed, may not have been the best of ideas.

Many people have, unfortunately, reported that reading these descriptions aloud while tripping created precisely what they were meant to dispel. By invoking the dark imagery while one was in such a sensitive and vulnerable state of consciousness, these images can spring to life. This understanding is extremely important to remember, because in addition to heightening the senses, dissolving psychological boundaries, and enhancing brain processes, LSD directly affects the architecture of one's belief system about the nature of reality. LSD is the most powerful tool ever invented for changing what we believe to be real, and this is why it is both cherished and feared by so many people.

An understanding of how one's set and setting can influence psychedelic mind states may be helpful in understanding this extraordinary book. In your hands is an utterly fascinating story about someone who bravely explored the darkest, most extremely hellish aspects of the human psyche on a quest for God, and returned to share his mind-bending story.

Hellucination takes the form of a page-turning memoir, combining personal trip reporting with science fiction, horror movie, and religious mythologies, philosophical speculation on the nature of the author's experiments with psychedelic drug combinations, strange encounters with other people who may not be what they seem, and the rationale behind his spiritual conversion from atheism to Christianity.

Underground film distributor and rare comic book dealer Stephen Biro's journey through the darkest depths of his personal and collective underworld is every bit as frightening, disturbing, and enlightening as any of the creepy creations in his vast DVD and comic book collections. A connoisseur of the weird, the bizarre, the sensational, and the horrific, Stephen filled his stores, his online inventories, his home, and his brain with the most profoundly gruesome imagery imaginable.

Then Stephen experimented with powerful, synergistic combinations of LSD, nitrous oxide, and cannabis, while watching ferocious movies, with dazzling special effects, on a quest for God. He watched psychedelic videos, The Matrix, Fight Club, and other violent and disturbing films on his entertainment center while taking massive amounts of psychedelics, mixing it with nitrous oxide. Not surprisingly, he had a series of hellish experiences, which he describes in great detail. The vivid and graphic visual descriptions in this book leave little to the imagination, and reading Stephen's memoir can seem like stepping inside one of H.R. Giger's macabre visionary paintings at times.

Psychiatric researcher Stanislav Grof's work with LSD demonstrated that the drug is basically a "nonspecific brain-amplifier." So when Stephen decided to experiment with LSD and other psychedelics he amplified the intensity of all this dark imagery and brought it to life.

Some of Stephen's extraordinary book Hellucination reminded me of my own attempts in Brainchild and Virus--the two semi-autobiographical science fiction novels that I've written--to describe psychedelic shamanic journeys that carried me from the underworld to the stars. I think that this journey from Hell to Heaven is an archetypal adventure, one that all human beings pass through when they take the path of psychedelic shamanism, and I also suspect that we are progressing through a similar pattern as a species.

Like Stephen, I've also personally experimented with psychedelic drugs quite a bit, and on some of my journeys, have had similar experiences to those that he describes in this book. However, while the conclusions that I drew from my own experiences were different, the archetypal dynamics and many of the motifs are similar, and they clearly resonate with the story line in Dante's Divine Comedy.

Religious or spiritual experiences are certainly not uncommon on psychedelics. Research by psychiatrist Oscar Janiger showed that people tend to have spiritual experiences on LSD around 24% of the time in a non-religious setting, that is, even when no spiritual or religious stimulus is present. When religious or spiritual stimuli are present, then the percentage can be much higher. Recent research at John Hopkins University in 2006 has demonstrated that psilocybin, the active ingredient in magic mushrooms, can produce religious or mystical experiences in 61% of its participants, which are in every way indistinguishable from those reported by mystics and religious figures throughout the ages.

However, although these studies shed some light on this unusual book, Biro never seemed to have a classic mystical experience on his psychedelic journeys.

In this mind-blowing book, Stephen experiences a progressive series of unbelievably bizarre personal hells, created, it appears, by filling his brain to the brim with dark and violent imagery while tripping--and this eventually propels him to break through into states of consciousness where he appears to meet and speak with "God." While encountering the presence of "God," or a higher spiritual intelligence, is not uncommon on high doses of psychedelics, Stephen's experiences stand out as truly unique among the reports that I've heard--like, for example, when he and the "real" "God" team up in hyperspace to violently kill and destroy the Western cultural "image" of "God."

4

If this weren't strange enough, as we progress further into Stephen's adventure, we learn that all of his encounters with "God" on psychedelics were really encounters with the Devil in disguise, or so Stephen comes to believe.

Much of the book describes how the voices of "God" and "the Devil"--in the author's own head, and coming through other people in various guises--are trying to win over his soul, and prevent him from succeeding in his spiritual quest. For Stephen, his experiences became clear and convincing evidence for a divinely-inspired belief system that corresponds with the Judeo-Christian Bible. Although I've had many profound spiritual experiences on psychedelics, I wasn't able to make this leap, and I still find myself surrounded by a universe of unfathomable mystery. Nonetheless, I absolutely loved Hellucination, and feel a resonance with its core message.

I completely loved the way that Stephen weaves his personal experience with the story lines from cool horror and science fiction films, and how vivid descriptions of his hellish acid trips become so extreme, so intense and over-the-top, that I would simultaneously squirm with fear and giggle with delight.

This can be a truly frightening book, and it is most definitely not for the faint-hearted. Hellucination is so frightening in certain sequences, because when you read it, you have no doubt that it is honest and authentic reporting. The nightmarish hells that Stephen experienced would scare the living daylights out of Edgar Allen Poe, H. P. Lovecraft, and Stephen King--and Stephen's mind-blowing story is his reality and a part of his life; that we are lucky he is willing to share with us.

But Hellucination can also be a pretty funny book at times, as Biro never loses his sense of humor, and sometimes his vividly-described hells can just become so damned horrible that they eventually become comical. For this reason, and because of the spiritual fruits that the author achieved, I actually found the book to be uplifting, as the hellish sequences often appeared to be grotesque parodies of my own life, and society at large, offering us fruitful opportunities for profound insight and thoughtful reflection.

--David Jay Brown

Author of "Mavericks of the Mind" and "Conversations on the Edge of the Apocalypse"

THE ID AND SUPEREGO ARE OUT OF THE SHADOWS

I exhaled, and the nitrous oxide soon exited my lungs. I sat on the couch—waiting—and I looked around the cramped apartment. Horror movie posters and bootleg videotapes surrounded me on all sides, in every crevice and between all the furniture.

I wasn't alone in the apartment.

I didn't want to see them, but they were both right there in front of me. They waited for my next move. Unsure of what to do, I spoke to the strongest of them.

"What the fuck are you doing? I can't live like this. I can't even carry on a normal conversation with you screaming at me all the time!"

He looked at me.

"You have to understand," he said. "Nobody is going to care about what you're experiencing now. They're too busy playing Xbox, deciding what TV shows to watch, worrying about getting laid tonight or otherwise grabbing a few happy moments so they don't have to think about their miserable lives."

"You do understand that, right?" he continued. "Everybody's lives are miserable to some degree or in some sense. Nobody can ever truly be happy without some sort of madness creeping into their souls."

I wanted to stand up and shout at him but instead, gave up. How can you compete with the devil? Your own personal Id? The part of yourself that wants to destroy you? So I continued to sit there for a moment, smoking like a chimney.

I turned to the part of myself supposed to give me guidance. He was standing in the corner, staring off into space. He gave the impression of being just like me—in fact, they both did. Sure, they wore better clothes and were clean shaven. But still me.

My Superego and my Id were made flesh. I've been screaming at them, pleading with them for longer than I want to admit. But they never changed. My

Superego—or, personal angel, as I came to consider him—didn't know what to say. I often begged for guidance, and only sometimes would I get it. Other times I got nothing. But my Id—my personal demon—knew exactly what to say. It knew how to manipulate me. It could even pretend it *was* me, masquerading as original thoughts growing inside my skull. But this time they weren't in my head. This time, they were external. I could finally see them standing in front of me.

So I screamed at my personal angel, "Say something! I'm counting on you to be my better half. How do I deal with his manipulations, his wanting to send me down the wrong path?"

My angel finally looked at me. I looked it up and down and locked gazes with its brown eyes—just like mine—as it spoke.

"You're doing what is right. You're doing what you need to do to find God, and if you keep knocking, he will have to answer you. Even the most horrendous sinners of this world will be answered if they knock long enough. Never stop until someone answers the door."

I gave a knowing sigh when my demon approached me. It said, "Listen to what this asshole is telling you—knock until your knuckles bleed and maybe, just maybe God might answer you! What kind of shit is that? I know who you are: You're nobody, a piece of crap that shouldn't have been born. You don't offer anything to this world. You just rape, steal, lie and screw others over. What makes you good enough to find God? Why would God answer you?"

A flash of evil spread across the demon's face as it leaned closer. I could see the hatred flare behind its pupils. My spine trembled, as its words were something I wasn't prepared for.

It said, "Many men and women—some very worthy—have tried to find God. They all failed. You are nobody. Nothing. And you're sure not what God wants."

I turned to my personal angel. "Is it true?"

It turned to me and said, "Ask, and it shall be given to you; seek, and you shall find; knock, and it shall be opened unto you."

Goosebumps covered my body as I stood up and yelled, "I need to know how long I'm supposed to knock, to search! I've ripped my mind apart, unleashing both of you."

My cigarette went out and I reached for another. I snubbed the filter in the ashtray and lit another in the time it took to take a breath. I looked at them both—not in the eyes, but rather at their feet. I didn't want to see too much of them anymore. I set the cigarette in the ashtray and let it smolder while I argued with these things, these extreme versions of myself.

"Fuck you both," I said. "Neither of you is helping me one bit."

I turned to the Id, daggers in my eyes.

"You not only do everything you can to destroy me—even disguising yourself as my actual thought processes—but you flip every good idea I have into something selfish and wrong. Your guile is beyond anything I can manage."

Before the Id could respond, I ripped into the Superego.

"And you speak in whispers. I can barely hear you because my demon is always drowning you out. It seems you can't be bothered to tell me the other side of the story. You only talk *after* my demon manipulates me! That doesn't protect me! If you sense my demon coming on, why don't you tell me what to do that is right? Why do you let me hear the wrong first?"

I continued shouting, directing my anger at both of them.

"Don't tell me Satan wins the first round in everything! I'm a human being, and if I'm in the middle of a war that is already given over to the Devil, because God is testing souls on some unknown criteria, then neither of you serve any purpose to me."

I flopped back down on the couch, and both sides of me stood there, momentarily speechless. My cigarette went out so I reached over to re-light it, while waiting for them to say something... anything.

It wasn't surprising which one spoke first. "Do whatever you want, Stephen. Just remember, better men have tried the road less travelled, and even they had to stray off it."

My personal angel fell to his knees, right before me. He clutched my legs and said, "Keep doing what's in your heart. It's a noble pursuit that many are not brave enough to undertake."

Their responses reinforced how frustrating my situation was. I was caught between the subtle machinations of the Hell-spawn or the delicate subterfuge of the Holy.

If that's even what these two really were. I decided to ask again.

"So you were both ripped from my mind simultaneously, battling for dominance inside my head? At first you lead me to believe you're God and the Devil before revealing yourselves as my personal angel and demon. And to make matters more confusing, you both show up looking like me. I don't know if you're merely two aspects of my mind or if you're actually angels and demons. Or maybe you're both demons doing some good cop, bad cop routine. Is this a game you play to win someone's soul? Or have I gone insane, and this is shit bleeding over into my normal reality? Hell, maybe I've died and this is Hell or Purgatory."

My Id laughed and said, "That's a lot of maybes, Steve. You still don't know what you've unleashed, but I will tell you this: You are not only in the middle of a war, but you've gone straight to the front lines—with no armor, no weapons and no clue as to how this is played. And you're fair game for everyone involved."

I took a deep breath and said, "You're right. I don't know what is going on but i have a gut feeling now. So I am going to keep searching because that is all that I can do."

I reached for the nitrous cracker and began filling it up in front of them. I was already on four hits of acid and my mind had split a long time ago. I didn't care. I just needed to escape—maybe search a little for God, maybe not.

"Let's see where this takes me," I thought. After four cartridges filled the balloon, I began to hit it like a joint.

I didn't consciously notice what was playing on TV but somehow felt it in the back of my mind. It was the "The Sandkings," a stupid *Outer Limits* episode about alien eggs brought down to earth and hatched by an ex-astronaut in his garage. The eggs produce alien spiders—actually two separate species—and, of course, one species was benevolent and one was evil. It paralleled my life at the moment. But even if I had been paying close attention to the television, I wouldn't have pondered the episode's significance to my life.

Because that's when it happened.

My two selves were no longer there. So I was alone in the apartment to witness the alien spiders become real. Five inches long, the multi-hued creatures began crawling from the TV, into my living room. At first, this was amazing to me, so I invited them in. But my attitude quickly changed when they kept coming. Five spiders turned into ten, ten turned into thirty, and thirty into hundreds. Suddenly, I had hundreds of flesh-eating otherworldly spiders crawling their way into my home.

I jumped up, worried the ravenous alien horde would engulf me. I ran towards my front door, inadvertently squishing a couple of them along the way. A sort of blue blood spurted from their crushed carcasses. I threw myself against the door and pushed spastically as the spiders proceeded to overrun the house.

I slammed against the door again, but it didn't budge. I was still pounding on it, terrified, when the spider horde began to swallow me. They climbed my body with terrifying speed. Even though this wasn't the first time something like this had happened, I was in a total panic, because I didn't know if it would be my last.

Three spiders clawed my face, and as I yanked them off, I felt their legs grip me harder. My flesh ripped wherever they had dug in. Then I felt spider fangs piercing through my clothes. All I could think of was venom—alien spider venom coursing through my veins, poisoning my body as it traveled through me.

I jumped back but was basically paralyzed with fear and indecision—and was being eaten alive! The spiders burrowed under my flesh, trying to get deeper into me. Blood began flowing freely from my body as more and more of them burrowed, bit and slashed.

An incessant stream of spiders entered my living room through the TV. They began fighting with each other out of intense hunger for flesh. I was that flesh, but there wasn't enough for all. I was still trying to rip them off of my body but was being vastly overwhelmed.

It seemed I had only one way left to escape: I had to jump through my window. So I ran for it, but my foot caught the edge of my love seat, and I flew towards the window with the momentum of the insane. I hit with a resounding crash.

The window comprised six small windowpanes separated by metal framing. I had hit it hard enough to break four panes, but the metal framing kept me from breaking through. I slammed back onto the love seat, but immediately jumped up, regretting my mistake. The spiders again attacked me in wave after wave.

I decided to try the front door again. This time, my desperate body somehow forced it to give, and I fell into the cold winter air.

I leaked blood like a sieve and wanted to scream, but I needed to check behind me in case my open doorway was allowing thousands of alien spiders to pour outside in pursuit. But they hadn't followed. I could see them still spilling out of the TV and crawling all over each other. I felt my mind spasm just a little, a fluctuation. Then a wave of energy erupted from me, dissolving the spiders in my apartment as if they were melting under intense heat.

I could see them liquefying, disseminating into nothingness as I tried desperately to regain my breath. I was finally able to inhale again, and I looked at my body. Every slash, rip and bit of mutilated flesh was gone. The blood, too, was mostly gone, but curiously, some of it remained.

Although I couldn't spot a single leftover spider, I was still wary. I walked onto my patio, hoping I'd feel safe there, but I didn't; my flesh crawled. I looked at my forearm and saw a huge gash. I poked it to see if it was real. The skin spread apart, oozing blood, and I knew it was real.

After checking around again to ensure I was still safe, I took a moment to consider my next action. It was pretty easy to figure out: When attacked by alien spiders, what's the sensible thing to do? Why, visit the hospital for some stitches, maybe get x-rayed for alien spider eggs beneath the skin. So that's exactly what I did.

Every inch of me checked out, and there wasn't a single alien spider egg under my skin. I only had the gash from the broken window, and I had that sewn up into a scar—eternal proof that I was attacked by alien spiders. Not that I need a physical reminder, I'll always remember that intense experience.

There's something else about this episode I'd really like to reveal to you. If I jumped ahead, I could tell you how this all makes sense, but I'd be ruining this memoir.

I can't yet tell you how I got here, or how I came to believe in the limits of our reality and the ability to bend it—how our minds can turn fantasy into reality or can be shaped and manipulated by unforeseen forces. These are the forces some might read about but most dare not touch; they turn away because the light is too bright.

But I'm inviting you in—starting from the beginning—because I need to tell it, and you hopefully want to know. To understand how one person has faith and another has nothing, it's helpful to know how I first lost my faith, my belief.

So let's start from the very beginning, and I do mean the *very* beginning...

BIRTH, DIVORCE AND CHILDHOOD TRAUMA

One cold February day, my parents decided to fuck. I have no assurance that the act they shared was one of love. More likely, it was the get-it-over-with, release sort of sex. My mother later confided that my father was a minuteman. So to my eternal shame, I was probably conceived in less than three minutes.

I know my parents were thrilled by my birth, because my mom had previously suffered a number of miscarriages. Twelve, to be exact. So it took thirteen tries to produce little ol' me! It's a little ominous, being number thirteen, so maybe it's not surprising I came out screaming.

I don't remember much about my early childhood, which is lucky for the reader, as I'm sure you'd rather be spared the details of what was, apparently, an early life stunningly uneventful. I remember some huge Styrofoam blocks that could be transformed into a castle, but that's about it.

My parents divorced when I was five. Mom later told me my father had been a wife beater and that she had been a slave to his manipulations. There are always two sides to a story, but I know from experience my dad had a temper that would put Hitler to shame. It's probably not fair, likening my dad to Hitler. But who says I have to be fair?

Most of my childhood memories are from after my mother moved away from Dad. My little sister and I lived in Ronkonkoma, New York with Mom. I was in the fourth grade and my sister was only three. I remember walking to the school bus stop, and I remember hanging out with friends. I'm not sure a fourth grader can really hang out, but I somehow managed it.

A couple older girls lived nearby, and I sometimes went to their houses to play. We had kissing contests, and I would squeeze their boobs as we smooched (or is this memory colored with wishful thinking?). They must have been at least 14, but I don't remember their names. I do recall breaking one of their beds while jumping on it. The bed damage got me kicked out of the house of the biggest-chested girl. Oh man, those boobs were big!

I also recall having a rock fight with some neighbor kids and pegging a girl in the forehead with a rock from about 25 yards away. Kids know enough not to get close during a rock fight, so when I hit her from such a distance I was simultaneously shocked and thrilled. At that age, I didn't realize the kind of damage a thrown rock could do to the human head. The girl ran home screaming, and I knew I was in trouble as I raced home to tell my mom. I've never felt a desire to physically hurt anyone, so I wasn't trying to do something dangerous. Later, when the girl's parents came over to complain, I learned she had needed seven stitches. "Stupid girl shouldn't have messed with a boy," I thought, showing myself to be a chauvinist pig at the tender age of eight! I felt bad she was hurt but felt little guilt, as I hadn't started the rock throwing. I just finished it. Nonetheless, I was sent to bed without supper (not such a bad deal; my bedroom was full of toys). In the end, I was forbidden from playing with that girl again.

Around the same time, I got a pair of shoes that seemingly enabled me to jump an extra ten feet off the ground. For hours, I jumped the bushes with that pair of shoes, believing every jump to be higher than the last. I know now that it wasn't quite as it seemed, but as a kid, that stuff sure felt real. It's something we lose as we get older: the magical ability of a child's mind to fuse reality and fantasy into a single experience. As we grow older, the re-evaluation of those magical feats is sobering; they may not have been as real as they seemed.

My father was a good-looking man. To me, he looked like a young Clint Eastwood, with similar hair, jawline, and features. He loved outdoor sports, and when he came to visit, we played outside and had a wonderful time. But on the downside, he was a major neat freak, a sort of Felix Unger clone from *The Odd Couple*. It really could make it hard to be together.

My harshest Dad memory occurred when he came to pick me up for a weekend once. He arrived in a huge green van he'd bought after the divorce. He was about three hours late, and I'd been excitedly waiting in the front yard all morning. I had even insisted on eating my PB&J sandwich in the driveway so I wouldn't miss him. When he pulled up, I jumped into the van and rushed into his arms to give him a huge hug. After my excitement settled, I got into the passenger seat and buckled my seatbelt, ready to go.

Then, for the first time this visit, my dad spoke: "Let me see your hands."

I looked at him, puzzled, as he lifted my hands. He saw dirty fingernails and went ballistic. He yelled for me to get out of his van and go back to my mother. He wasn't going to take a dirty kid with him. I begged and pleaded, and when Mom came to the car to bring my sister, angry words erupted between my parents.

I ran into the house, crying, and found solace under the bedcovers. Mom tried to console me but the wound had been inflicted and would never fully heal. My dad rejected me because of dirty fingernails, and because I only saw him twice a month then, this was majorly traumatic. The divorce had been especially hard on my mother and me (my lucky little sister hadn't a clue what divorce was), and it was, while crying under the bedcovers that I realized the divorce had been my fault; my father had wanted to get away because I was dirty.

From that point on, I blamed myself for everything. And that's when my nightmares started. I was soon taken to a psychologist and treated for being a nightmare-haunted, eight-year-old chauvinist who caused his parents' divorce.

It was a painful period, so I'll not re-open too many old wounds. Though I didn't recognize it at the time, my mother was suffering from bi-polar disorder. Over the next few years, her condition worsened and she struggled to care for my sister and I. As children we enjoy a temporary ignorance from the pains of adulthood, so I was unaware of the heartache my mother was experiencing. Children watch their parents do crazy shit and wonder, "Why are they doing this?" Little do their innocent minds comprehend how miserable adult life can be.

Mom had a close girlfriend who had three boys from a previous marriage. Let's call her "Rebecca," and the boys were, say, "John," "Jacob" and "Asshole." The boys were all blonde and fair skinned while Rebecca sported a blonde beehive hairdo. They were truly horrible kids and used to beat the shit out of me to ease their pain of not having a dad. I didn't understand this at the time. All I understood was the weekly ass kicking I received from Asshole. John was five, and Jacob was my age. Asshole was twelve and beefy. Perfect bully size.

The worst beating I took from Asshole was during the winter of 1976. We were having a jovial snowball fight until Asshole got hit in the face by an icy projectile thrown by one of his brothers. For some reason, Asshole reacted by charging me and punching me on every conceivable spot on my body. Punching, kicking and jumping on me, he pummeled my body deep into the snow on the side of the road.

It felt like the beating lasted 15 minutes. Scratch that. It felt like the beating lasted a lifetime. I vaguely remember his brothers standing around, egging him on as he trounced me.

What I didn't know at the time was that Asshole was infatuated with the eponymous pugilist of the recently released *Rocky*. He had apparently seen the film five times in the theater. He would constantly dance around singing that stupid freaking theme music, and he always sang it while stomping my head into the snow. I hadn't seen *Rocky* at the time and at first didn't realize that his singing of the theme meant an ass kicking was forthcoming. But I eventually learned that Asshole's rendition of "Dun du du duh du du dun dun dunnn" meant for me to scram. Even today, I can't hear the *Rocky* theme without feeling a twinge of panic.

Luckily, Mom's relationship with her friend became strained and they moved away. So ended my weekly ass beatings.

My mother was dating several guys at once, and they each had their own approach towards her and us kids. The nicest one was named Frank. He taught me how to carve a ring out of a peach pit and was always supportive and easygoing. He was a big man with a bushy beard. I wished my Mom would have kept him around.

Momentarily jumping ahead to the present, with your indulgence: My Mom recently died from cancer, and a couple of months before she left us, she began wanting to find Frank through the Internet, saying it was a huge mistake to have let him go. I felt bad for her as she talked about him. He must have been a genuinely good guy to be remembered on her deathbed. Past regrets can come bubbling up when the end is near. It's something many of us will have to face someday. Could've, would've, should've—those words haunt many people, not only in death but in life.

Jumping back to age eight: While rooting around for lost change, I made a discovery under the cushions of the living-room couch. If I had known the word at the time, I might have called my discovery "kinky." Most would simply call it disturbing. I had fished a magazine out of the couch and had immediately recognized it as an adult thing. I checked to see that the coast was clear and made a mad dash to my bedroom. I closed the door, jumped on my bed and began leafing through it.

Ironically, I don't remember what the magazine was called. But I can vividly recall each and every sordid page in it. It was a porno magazine about a woman who, while walking through the park, is abducted by two men, bound and raped on a park bench. This being the 1970s, rape and bondage publications weren't illegal and had become a staple of the new adult industry that was just emerging.

The text was printed on the side of the pages, next to the pictures, and represented the woman's thoughts as she was being raped. It mesmerized me, and my immature mind turned it into an obsession. I read it every day as soon as I returned home from school.

I read and re-read every page about this woman, who was just minding her own business when two masked men grabbed her and took her to a remote park bench. She kept thinking to herself, "Oh my God! I'm going to be raped, and I have no control over it!" The abductors tied her up in different bondage positions and took her at the same time. After they finished their second orgasm each, they left her tied to the bench, and she's left alone with her thoughts and actually begins to romanticize the situation, considering herself fortunate to have been chosen by the two men who desired her purely for her sexuality.

Behind closed doors and in total awe, I soaked in these images and descriptions. I didn't know anything about what adults do (the birds-and-bees talk was a ways off), but I nonetheless took a crash course in the advanced subjects of rape, bondage, threesomes and cumplay. Too young to know it was fake, I was surely warping my impressionable psyche with this rape mag, so maybe it was just was well that Mom eventually busted me with it and took it away.

I think the mag was left by a boyfriend of hers named Saul who had a mirror business. Saul seemed like an okay guy. My Mom worked for him and they dated for a couple of months. He then disappeared along with her job. In the good ol' days, you could fuck your employees and coworkers without the worry of a sexual harassment lawsuit. It just takes a couple of assholes to ruin the party. And there are always assholes.

Around then, in the fourth grade, some idiot farted next to me in class and blamed me for it. We'll call this troublemaker "Chris." The very picture of '70s hot stuff, Chris came to school wearing silk disco shirts that made my Garanimals look more childish than they already were (you may remember Garanimals as the color-coded clothes that kids used to match their shirts and pants all by their lonesomes). Chris listened to KISS, and I had no clue what or who KISS was.

Anyway, after this dickhead blamed the fart on me, I was christened "Whiff!" The Whiff I was, and anyone who farted in school could point their finger my way. And how those little fuckers pointed! I was actually a good sport about it. Hated it but never broke down over it.

But it reached a new level of humiliation when a little shit named Alex wrote a story about "The Whiff Family" and was allowed to read it to the whole class. His two-page story ridiculed me and my family to the juvenile delight of my classmates. Alex's pen had transformed my Mom into "The Whiff Monster"—a creature who served fart balls for dinner to our family in our garbage-can dwelling. I sat in secret mortification, but sadly, I had to laugh along with everyone else because it was my only option. Even the teacher seemed to be getting a kick out of the story, which frightened me because I counted on her to put a stop to this. She knew I had been made into a walking joke by my nickname, but it didn't seem to matter to her. No, the only reprieve from humiliation came when that bastard Alex finally finished his opus. The adult in charge was supposed to protect the innocent—why didn't that happen and why did she give him an A?

The Whiff name stuck until this girl named Michelle puked in the hallway while waiting for lunch. Fortunately for me, puke trumps a fart, and she became Puke Michelle. I gratefully drifted out of the limelight.

There were some good times and more bad times.

Soon, my mother's depression landed her in the hospital. Before she left, she introduced me to our new, unofficial guardians: John and Cheryl. I wasn't clear on where my mother had met these two; for all I know, it was through a classified ad.

Cheryl was pregnant, and John was a long-haired hippie type. The first thing I noticed about him was he was dirty and unwashed. I wasn't yet a great judge of character, but I knew dirt. Young boys are experts on the subject. Ask any kid, and he will, at the very least, be able to describe the stuff in his front yard with great detail. Hell, I can even remember the taste of our neighbor's dirt. I was that much of a dirt hobbyist.

This new family unit all sat around the big, discarded electrical wire spool that served as the kitchen table. My little sister was still with us, but I barely remember seeing her. I don't know why. I should be able to tell you a lot more about her from that time, but I can't. Wish I could.

Before Mom had left, John told me all about the football we would play and other fun we would have, spouting anything he could to reassure Mom feel better about leaving us kids with a couple of strangers.

I got a life lesson when Mom left: Just because someone says something... well, that doesn't make it so. After Mom left for the hospital, er, "vacation," I didn't play football or have any other fun with John and Cheryl. Instead, I got beaten and kicked while being used as a slave to fetch cheese sandwiches and drinks for their friends. I was abused for their amusement. Things were thrown at me as if I was a fucking unpaid carnival sideshow freak.

I also remember Cheryl lying on my Mom's bed having her belly rubbed by two guys in a sexual way. I watched for a couple of minutes before they saw me. The door was slammed in my face.

This sort of behavior lasted a couple of months, until my uncle showed up unexpectedly. He freaked out when he found a huge bag of pot on the living room table. He tried to kick out all the dirty hippies, and it got ugly fast—even more intense when the police arrived. Some of the hippies split but John was arrested and Cheryl was evicted.

My mom returned from the hosp-, er, "vacation," and that's when the threats and harassment started. We lived in a wooded area so the hippie clan could come from out of nowhere to screw with us, and they did. I guess they were some kind of gang. Cheryl came back to threaten us and got arrested. She screamed that her hippie cohorts would kill us. "They'll make you pay!" Also around that time, John was arrested again for trying to break down the front door with some of his friends.

That period remains a blur of images and emotions that confuse me. I suppose I could give more details, but I don't want to remember. There was more to it—there always is—but let's keep it at that, huh?

Shortly after, Mom went into the hospital again, so my father took us in. The house we had been living in was a shambles, and my paternal-side family was afraid our belongings were infested with cockroaches or disease. So we ended up leaving our stuff behind and I lost almost all my possessions. The whole of my father's clan were germ-o-phobes beyond reason. I'm not. I believe a little floor spice helps keep the immune system on its toes. My father's paranoid side of the family tree tried to scare me. Scarred is more like it.

I was allowed to keep a small box of *Mad, Crazy* and *Cracked* magazines, but only after it had been sprayed with untold amounts of bug spray. Anytime I removed an issue from this box, I got high from insecticide fume remnants. I had collected humor mags every time I came across one, but Dad threw hundreds away; I could only keep what fit in that small box.

So began life with Father. Looking back, this was a short chapter in my life but a big one

MY FIRST CHILDHOOD STEP TOWARDS ATHEISM

My father was a good man but very set in his ways. He never drank or smoked. He was an exercise junkie who ate healthy food. And when I say healthy, I mean a "soy beans, granola bars and salads with the occasional peanut butter sandwich for lunch and once-a-week baked chicken with a salad"-type of healthy. This doesn't sound too bad, but this was our diet in its entirety. And this was the '70s! What's more, the treat of baked chicken was only consumed in the winter. My father's colon must have been smooth enough to host the Olympic toboggan finals, and every team would break the previous year's world record.

If we had to eat out on the road, it was Burger King, home of the mother-fucking Whopper. Why? Because it was flame broiled and not fried in its own fat. Ah, what used to pass for a selling point to the health conscious; as I'll say many times: the '70s were a different time. In any case, we ate healthily and did a lot of sports.

My sister and I traveled with Dad as Mom was busy cracking up. As he searched for a job that could support us all, we went from New York to Florida, Florida to California (with a layover in Texas), up to Colorado and back to New Jersey. It was an amazing time. My dad's big, green van was our room on wheels. We had plenty of legroom and plenty of peanut butter sandwiches. Some nights we stayed at motels and others we slept in the van. Luckily for us, my Dad used our college fund (left for us by his folks) and instead spent the money on amusement parks and all the Big Red Gum we asked for. He never really found any work so we ended up back in New Jersey.

Looking back, I think it was all a ruse to show us some fun—show us the country while trying to make up for life without Mom. It worked. One of the trip's highlights happened in Colorado. We were driving up the side of a mountain on a winding road that bordered some sheer cliffs. Peering over the side, you saw nothing but blackness beyond the guard rails.

We reached the top, and as we started our descent on the other side, we ran out of gas. My dad cursed and told us to buckle our seat belts since we were going to have to coast all the way down. I was ecstatic. It felt as if we were free falling down this narrow two-lane mountain road, and I was transfixed by the view down the precipitous side. It was snowing, and my dad started to count off mile markers. He reached at least 20, and we coasted for over 30 minutes.

At the bottom of the hill was a hotel, and we whipped into the parking lot and rolled to a slow stop. A couple people ran out of the hotel and told us to come inside quickly; a bear had just attacked a dog in the area. This was even more exciting than the coasting, and when we woke the next morning, we learned the bear was trapped in a cage that had been set up during the night. Colorado was exciting!

During this trip, I formed a set of beliefs that would stay with me for a long time. I was in the back seat of the van when I asked my Dad if he believed in God. He turned around and told me, point blank, without a blink or trace of a smile on his face, "I won't believe in God until he comes up to me and taps me on the shoulder."

I was shocked and a little dismayed. I attended church a couple of times with Mom but religion was never explained to me. I think it's difficult for parents to explain religion or God to their kids, worried they might fuck the kids up with some wrong answers. Church with Mom without any explanations had left me curious.

Dad was the smartest guy I knew so I valued his opinion. And if he didn't believe in God, then God must not exist. I mean, Dad had been on the planet a lot longer than I. My mom had never told me anything about Him, and I had no concept of her beliefs. So from that day, I started proclaiming I didn't believe in God.

My new atheism didn't stem from any reasoning on the matter but merely because of Dad's beliefs. While it's important for parents to have The God Talk with their kids, it should be open-ended enough that no inadvertent brainwashing occurs. After all, beliefs are very personal and a true choice in this life. Kids are very impressionable and swayed by their parents but they still have to make the choice in their life.

Dad found a job in New Jersey, and he registered me back into the fourth grade. I had been taken from Mom before completing the grade and had to repeat it. I started this school with a clean slate and began a better life in new surroundings. No Whiff here!

Classes were unremarkable except for the English periods. I fell in love with my English teacher, whose name I forget. Sporting her salt-and-pepper bouffant hairdo and black horn-rimmed glasses, she got her students excited about reading and the classics. She wasn't a paycheck teacher, she got satisfaction out of sharing knowledge. I've been lucky enough to be taught by three such teachers in my life.

School was good, and I was having fun developing an interest in bicycle motor cross, more commonly known as BMX. All my friends had Redlines and Mongooses with Tuff Wheel 2's and alloy seat poles and chromies for their tires. I didn't have a bike but was a good rider from my time spent on borrowed bikes. And after much pleading, my Dad agreed to buy one for me, but he was only willing to shop at Toys R Us. They didn't have a good selection, but the Huffy Bandit caught my eye. That model may not have gone down in the annals of cool-bike history, and I don't know how long they were in production, but it was certainly the best bike I could find at a toy store. The handlebars twisted up and back (much like a ten-speed but in the opposite direction) while the frame attempted some wannabe futuristic detailings, with extra chunks of metal in odd places. And the tires? Well, they were wild looking, with a half-inch rubber section in the middle, which tapered away into square knobbies that looked like they would grip the dirt for the ultimate traction on a turn. (The tires actually gave no traction, despite their crazy design, and I ended up on my ass more times than I liked.)

I was so happy and proud to have my first real bike. As soon as Dad finished assembling it, I wanted to show it off to my friends. Boy, was that a mistake.

I peddled excitedly to a wooden ramp my friends had just made. I pulled up to them with a skid worthy of my cool new bike. To my surprise and disappointment, they laughed their asses off.

"What the fuck is that?"

"Is that thing held together with plastic?"

"Look at those wheels! Look at those wheels!"

I kept insisting, "No, guys, it's a cool bike!" They laughed even harder.

So I backed up and pumped the pedals hard towards the ramp. I had to show them a thing or two about the fucking Huffy Bandit! I soared through the air and landed a great distance past the jump ramp. They stopped laughing. Apparently I had laid down the gauntlet: "Okay, let's jump for distance."

So we jumped the Hell out of that ramp, and the Huffy Bandit performed surprisingly well against the Redlines and Mongooses. But jumping ramps and creeks and everything else with the BMX kids took a heavy toll on my new bike. I snapped the frame almost in half. My father knew welding, so he soon had it roadworthy again. Over the next months, he welded that bike so many times it slowly became a pure-metal beast that weighed more than I did.

My sister and I lived with Dad for about two years. We were latchkey kids because he worked a lot, sometimes until late at night. We filled our time with episodes of *Love Boat* and *Fantasy Island*.

We lived in a two-bedroom apartment, so my sister had her own room, and Dad and I shared the other. I had half the room, and Dad had the other half. My Dad was dating at the time, and in retrospect, I realize I was cramping his style. How could he bring women home, with me sleeping on a twin bed a few feet away? I can only hope some of those "late nights at work" actually had him out getting some tail.

My dad taught me frugality, showing me how a dollar could be stretched beyond its normal limits. He was a saver and a fixer. He could fix anything, and everything had its place. In our spotless room, I had a single shelf for my things that I kept clean and tidy—too tidy. I think that's why I later became a slob. Hell, I *know* that's why. "Take that Dad! I just threw my dirty underwear into the microwave!" (I actually did stick my underwear in the freezer once. Ah, the wonders of ice-cold underwear in the dead heat of summer...)

My sister frequently got me into trouble by blaming me for stuff she did, and we had all the other usual brother-sister squabbles. She would hit me and I would hit back, then she'd rat on me, and I'd get into trouble. She hit first, but I hit harder, and she would get pissed off.

RELIGIOUS MISHANDLINGS AND WALKING DOWN THE WRONG PATH

Dad worked hard but ended up hurting his back pretty badly. He needed surgery so couldn't take care of us anymore. We had basically been on the lam with him anyway, since our mom had legal custody of both of us. We hadn't heard a thing from her and maybe would have been featured on a milk carton if they'd been doing that back then. After getting out of the hospital, Mom had married a guy named Tom and ended up in Chicago. Tom was a real piece of work, I would discover.

Dad got in touch with Mom, and she was thrilled to take us both back. She and Tom were in the middle of moving to South Carolina where Tom had taken a job. They already had a house picked out. So Dad packed us up, and off to SC we went. I looked forward to being with my Mom again since I thought Dad was such a hardass. I think a lot of children of divorce must do this: worship the parent that doesn't have custody. That is, until they're back living with them. "Grass is greener," whatnot. But we moved back in with Mom and life was good.

I soon had my first South Carolina girlfriend, but nothing happened between us—not even a kiss. A shame, because other boys told me she was a slut who liked kissing.

School was a breeze. I got all A's since the schools in the South seemed way behind those in the North. When I was in the sixth grade, I felt as if I was doing fifth-grade lessons.

I fished and explored the woods. Since we lived in the boonies, those were the basic entertainment options. My mom and stepfather had a wonderful German Shepherd named Shotzie. She was my best friend, and she accompanied me on all the exploring, fishing, and fun.

My parents were members of a nearby church, and they became good friends with the pastor, who frequently dropped by for drinks and dinner. The church building was a doublewide trailer, and we attended a service every other Sunday. We sat on foldable metal chairs, and after falling asleep once while leaning back in one of those chairs, I woke to a loud crash with the whole congregation staring at me. "I'm glad you could join us Stephen," intoned the Minister. Humiliated, I picked up my chair and pretended to immerse myself in the service with copious deliveries of "Amen" and "Hallelujah!"

This church was creepy to me. They spoke in tongues, waved their hands around, and generally spazzed out. All that shaking and Holy Ghost-type seizures were traumatic to the kid who didn't understand the rituals. And I had no clue what was happening (remember, my Mom wasn't much on explaining religion).

But it gets really twisted. Understand, my stepfather was an accomplished alcoholic, and by "accomplished" I mean he could function while drunk. He could handle a decent job for about a year or two before getting fired. Then he was off to the next company. Being an alcoholic means having alcoholic friends, so that explains the minister and his wife making constant appearances at our house. I'd been to their house, met their kids and had some fun times. But the fun ended one night, as they dropped a bomb that helped reinforce the anti-religion beliefs Dad had fostered in me.

It started as a normal visit from the pastor and his wife—just drinking with my parents. The booze was flowing freely, and I was floating around the house as usual, only sometimes listening to the adults talk. But then I was riveted when I overheard the visiting couple tell my folks they had something important to confess. It sounded heavy, so I sat my happy ass down on the couch, keeping my body flush against the sofa so nobody would realize I was there. Although the conversation had obviously turned serious, I wasn't nearly prepared for what I was about to hear.

Sobbing, the pastor and his wife revealed they had been seducing neighborhood children and teenagers. As they confessed to tawdry threesomes and foursomes, I initially had wishful, prurient thoughts about being a seduction victim, as the wife was pretty hot. Mom and Tom—aghast—tried to get the couple to leave our house. But the pastor and wife had a strong need to unburden themselves, and the confessions kept on coming. The alcohol was a serum that brought out some ugly truths that night.

After my parents finally ousted their visitors, they argued about which one of them had wanted to join the church. They seemed on the verge of a huge fight when they noticed me sitting on the couch. My mom asked if I'd been there the whole time. Without waiting for an answer, she ordered me to bed. They were both pretty drunk, so I made it to my room without further conversation. I closed the door but tried, in vain, to continue following the conversation in the other room. I flopped down on my bed and thought about

24

how fucked up it all was. I was just starting puberty and feeling the tug of manhood but didn't know what to do. The hotness of the minister's wife, with her tight dresses and high heels, was exciting. Yet the fantasy was destroyed, as the pastor was an old man with a white-haired Elvis pompadour.

I still didn't know much about religious beliefs, but I knew the minister had some power over people. That power, at least over my family, had been destroyed in a single drunken conversation. We never returned to that church or saw them again. I don't know their names; I don't even know exactly where the church was (we were living in nearby Gaffney, South Carolina). I'm sure they ended up getting arrested eventually because stuff like that can't remain secret when children are involved. I just hope and pray they stopped abusing kids right after those confessions.

These shocking events helped keep me in the Atheism camp. But my mom and step-dad just pretended it never happened, and mom went in search of another church.

She found a Mormon one that wasn't bad. The same kind of rituals were performed, but it wasn't in a doublewide, and hopefully the minister wasn't screwing his neighbors' kids. Everything went fine until my mother wanted me to be baptized. I had already been baptized Lutheran as a baby, but Mom insisted I be baptized into the Mormon faith. I was to have my sins washed away and become a Mormon. I don't think a sixth grader has that many sins darkening his soul, but what the hell? My Mother wanted it, and if it made her happy, I was game.

So when the day came, I was dressed in all white and taken to church to get my baptism on, Mormon style. (That almost sounds dirty, doesn't it? "Mormon style." I figure one sense of that term would mean three quick pumps in missionary and it's over. But then again, you'd have more than one wife. So it would be three pumps here, five pumps there and maybe ten pumps into the last one. To tell the truth, I've never seen a Mormon have sex, but I don't think I'd want to. Not kinky enough for me, even with the multiple wives.)

In any case, I was standing in church with five other kids with the eyes of the congregation on us. I was third in line to get dunked and was nervous, mainly because of the crowd. When the praying and singing started, the first kid was led to a large white tank surrounded by white tiles. While the priest or minister or whatever he was (I forget the Mormon terminology) continued to pray, he dunked the kid in the water and pronounced him baptized. Everyone clapped and praised Jesus, or whoever it is that Mormons praise (I told you I'm not good with this Mormon stuff).

The next kid walked to the tank, and the singing and praising continued. Then he was dunked and saved. I didn't know any of the other boys, and the whole thing seemed weird, but I was only a sixth grader, so what did I know?

The organist played, the people sang, and it was my turn to march towards the dunking tank. The minister kept ranting, and I wanted to curl up in a ball of self-consciousness. I walked calmly into this oversized bathtub and stood next to the minister/priest/whatever as I waited for him to dunk me.

The music and ranting stopped. He held me by the back, laid his hand on my head, and said, "Do you take Jesus Christ as your personal savior and now belong to the Mormon faith?"

"I do," I whispered.

He started mumbling some other stuff and suddenly dunked me in the water. I wasn't ready because he had done it so quickly. The water rushed up my nose and down my throat and I began gasping and thrashing around until he lifted me to pronounce me saved.

But he didn't.

He looked at the congregation, then me and said, "Not all of your hair submerged, so you're not saved yet. Let's do it again."

It's damned annoying when you're not saved because of a mistake on the clergy's end, but I stood there quietly. He went through his spiel again and dunked me a second time. Chlorinated water went right back up my nose, and I again flailed my arms, desperate to breathe.

He raised me and gave me a look. He turned to the congregation and said, "It happened again. We have to totally submerge him so he can be fully baptized."

I panicked as he shoved me back under the water. I can only imagine what the congregation was thinking: "Surely he's the Devil's spawn, and that's why he can't be baptized." I was choking and splashing as the minister/priest/sadist pulled me back up.

"All of your hair still didn't get wet," he said in disbelief. But he was finished, and he shook his head. He pronounced me baptized in a weary voice, and the organist pounded on the keys. I struggled out of the tub, humiliated and confused.

Was I baptized or not? If the baptism didn't take because of some dry hair, and if the holy man just gave up on me, was I going to Hell? Even though I considered myself an atheist, my almost-adolescent mind was fretting on the matter for weeks afterwards. If that asshole would have dunked me good and proper, I would have been saved a ton of grief.

This Mormon near-drowning seemed to give me another reason to follow my dad's advice about belief in God. That's a fucking shame, and I can only guess how many religious people have shattered a child's faith. On the one hand, it's a fucked-up irony that religion can destroy the very seeds of faith. But on the other hand, maybe it's to be expected—religion is man's business towards God, and man is nothing if not fallible. Gross misdeeds, fits of greed, and other human failings are bound to fuck up any religious system in the long run. But even if explained by human imperfection, the mishaps of religion still constitute a juicy target for atheists.

Soon afterward, my stepfather was fired for being drunk at work, and we moved to Nebraska, where he had found work at a beef processing plant. We lived in a town of 296 people. I know the exact population because it was written on a sign at the edge of town. The town was Jacksonville, and it was in the middle of nowhere.

Talk about small. I was in a class of ten kids, and this was the combined seventh and eighth grades. Both grades were mostly girls ("Can I hear an Amen!").

The class had a teacher who loved his job, but here, it was roughly a sixth-grade curriculum in the seventh grade. I wasn't challenged, as I already learned it all the previous year in South Carolina (and as I've mentioned before, the sixth grade in South Carolina was New Jersey's fifth grade; I'm not exaggerating, although I wish I were).

So I was one of three boys in a sea of seventh- and eighth-grade girls. The other two guys were genuine rednecks (buck teeth on one, two silver front teeth on the other), and I was the new city-slicker kid everyone wanted to know about (I got to play New Kid in South Carolina too, but with only ten kids in my Nebraska classroom, it was a lot more interesting). All the girls were pretty, but I still had no clue how to make a move, so I didn't fool around.

We lived there for about a year. I enjoyed being the jock and the go-to guy for answers, but it was boring in the middle of nowhere unless you had a motorbike. I began to save for one, because I seemed to be the only guy in town without either a motorbike or a three-wheeler.

Tired of everyone zooming past as I walked around town on two boring ol' legs, I became more enterprising and accelerated my savings by picking up occasional odd jobs. Mowing lawns, raking leaves, washing cars. Most neighbors turned me down, but I persisted until I managed to save about $300. I was getting close to that motorbike.

Around this time, I realized the extent of my step-dad's alcoholism. He was always stumbling around drunk, but he wasn't mean. He was a nice drunk. I got home from school one day to find Mom and Tom really excited about something.

"Stephen," they said. "We have a surprise for you in the garage. Go see what it is."

I rarely got gifts, so I excitedly rushed to the garage. Inside was a pedal-driven moped with a bow on it. I looked at it confusedly.

"What is that?"

"It's a moped, honey. We took your money and bought it for you! We figured your step-dad could make a more informed purchase and negotiate a better deal than a kid could."

27

I was flabbergasted.

"You took my money and bought me a moped? How am I supposed to drive that thing with my friends in the woods?" It was true. We were in the boonies, surrounded on all sides by dirt, a surface that can't be negotiated by a moped. Mom looked at Tom, who was beginning to get a little sloppy from his latest round of drinks.

"Come to think of it, why *did* you get a moped?" she asked.

"Well, I was talked into it by the guy. It's German engineering, you know. Anyway, I can't take it back now."

I made the best of it, but driving in the snow was horrible, and it was impossible to keep up with my friends' dirt bikes and three wheelers. I was the laughingstock of the streets, but I was used to the feeling. And what's more, I could hit 30 miles an hour and get 50 miles to the gallon.

I lived next to Kevin, and we would play baseball or Atari video games at my house. My family had the only Atari in the neighborhood at that time. We also had one of the first VCRs, as my stepdad had stolen it from his Sears engineering workplace. The VCR and Atari were downstairs in the basement, which was my magical, secluded place of video games and R-rated HBO programming. Life as a seventh grader seemed like Heaven, and I was just about to discover a new basement pastime.

Understand: Back then, I had a knack for picking locks. Give me a coat hanger or a library card, and I was in. And we had two extra rooms in the basement. One was a laundry room where my mother stored her canning supplies (canning was a common practice for women in snowy Nebraska), and the other was my stepfather's storage room.

Predictably, since his storage room was off limits to all of us, I knew there were forbidden treasures in there. So I jimmied the door one night, after everyone had gone to bed, and I looked around. It was a mess, stuff strewn about everywhere, but I noticed a fireproof safe in one corner and a shelf in another. I walked over to the shelf and inspected the several videotapes on it.

Even if the videos had been mainstream cinema, I would have been thrilled. The local video store was 40 miles away, and we only made that trek once a week. The video store only had 300 films or so in their collection. This was when VHS was new, and barely anything had been released. So I was really excited to have some different videos.

I picked up the tapes and noticed the titles: *Debbie Does Dallas*, *Little Girls Blue* and *Cherry Truckers*. I didn't yet know exactly what I held in my hands. I'd seen some pseudo-naughty films on cable that had gotten my heart beating a little faster. The Internet hadn't been invented, and my main exposure to pornography had been in magazines. As has become my mantra already in this book: The '70s were a different time. In any case, I thought I merely had naughty booby movies in my hand.

I took the videotapes into the basement den and instinctively hid two of them under the couch. I turned off the lights and slid *Debbie Does Dallas* into the VCR. The Caballero logo appeared with a nice thrumming sound as if it were one of the big studios. Believe it or not, I was contemplating popcorn when the first trailer started. By the time the trailers finished, I had seen hot model-looking chicks naked ... and sucking ... and getting fucked ... and threesomes ... and cum shots—all on regular 35mm film. My mind spasmed, and popcorn was no longer on my mind.

When the title told me "The Main Feature Is About to be Presented," I ran up the stairs and locked the basement door. My eyes were glued to the screen during *Debbie Does Dallas*, and for some odd reason, my pants didn't fit any longer. Tight pants or not, it was the beginning of a beautiful friendship. My new friend Porn was always there for me, almost daily, for several months. Then my stepfather discovered what I was up to and hid the videos in the ceiling of his bedroom.

My last sentence should indicate I knew the videos' new secret hideout. I removed them from the ceiling and replaced them after each time I had, ahem, "hung out" with new buddy Porn. Months later, he was wise to me again and put them in his fire safe. Perhaps he noticed I hadn't rewound them to the exact same spot. But I had a paperclip and determination and was soon watching *Little Girls Blue* again. I think any boy with raging hormones would have done the same. Porn had been locked away in an airtight safe and longed to escape and hang out with the hot-blooded boy with the diamond-hard dick.

So life in Nebraska was good, especially down in the basement. I think I must have been shooting out knee cartilage after a while.

I got into the occasional spot of trouble in Jacksonville. Kevin had a slingshot, and we were hunting birds one day. We followed a couple of pigeons back to an abandoned building filled with old cars, records and arcane devices from the '30s and '40s. We walked through a hole in the wall and shot at the birds. I managed to shoot four pigeons and Kevin shot three. We picked up their limp bodies, thinking of bringing them home for our moms to cook. They had huge breasts on them, so when I brought them home, my Mom was actually excited. She began dressing them when there was an angry knock on the door.

The angry knocker was the proprietor of the local gas station. He was pissed and was asking about the slaughter of the breeding pigeons in his barn. I looked at him and plainly said, "I did it. I didn't know that was your barn; I thought it was abandoned."

He was amazed. "My daughter saw you boys leave the barn. I already asked the other boy, and he denied it. But you had the guts to own up to your actions." My Mom was upset, so I said, "How can I make up for it?"

He laughed and said, "I suppose you can work at my garage for a couple of weeks."

"Yes sir."

I didn't get in trouble from Mom, but she did throw away the pigeon breasts. I went by the garage right after school. I worked there a couple of weeks, schlepping stuff around and sweeping the driveway.

Wanting to be closer to Tom's job, we prepared to move to South Sioux City, which borders Sioux City, Iowa but is still in Nebraska. I had three weeks to go before graduating. We had a big baseball game with all the kids in town, and I was playing first base. My friend Kevin was pitching, something at which he was not known to excel. Everyone was getting pissed because he couldn't even put the ball close to the plate, much less anyone allowing for hits or strikes. The other kids were clamoring for me to take over on the mound. Kevin kept telling them to shut up, and he kept pitching the ball 15 feet from the plate. As everyone kept begging for me to pitch, the silver-toothed Kevin got frustrated and pitched worse and worse. One of the guys got hold of the ball and threw it to me, telling me to relieve Kevin.

That's when my friend lost it. He became a fucking maniac, grabbing an aluminum bat and charging me, swinging at my head. Running in circles as if chased by a serial killer, I yelled to my friends to throw *me* a bat. Nobody did, and that may have been a good thing. So I kept running, and after Kevin announced he was going to kill me, I decided to run to my house, which was very near the field. I couldn't run straight into my house so I went towards the fence.

Kevin caught up with me, took a swing and connected with my kneecap. I went down hard.

"You fucking psycho! What the fuck is wrong with you!"

He lifted the bat high into the air, and it was poised to crack my skull open. My mother suddenly appeared and grabbed the bat away from him as he began his death blow.

"What the fuck are you doing?" she screamed.

Kevin ran towards his home, next door. I was clutching my knee and Mom suggested we go to the hospital.

The cops weren't called because, well, that's how we played it back then. I was given a splint and told to stay off my leg for a little while. I couldn't return for the last several weeks of school since the building had its share of staircases, and I had a class on the fifth floor. I was passed anyway since I was at the top of the curve. We moved to South Sioux City three weeks later.

There, my stepdad received his fifth or sixth DUI (yes, drivers could get that many back then without license revocation). Mom and Tom's marriage began to deteriorate faster than before. The drinking was out of control, and my Mom secretly saved money to leave him. Soon we were packing for Florida, where my Mom's parents lived.

My grandparents didn't like me because I grew my hair long, and my sister and I grew even further apart. We moved several times and settled in Tarpon, Florida.

* * *

I'll conclude the "growing up in the '70s" portion of the memoir here. Hopefully, you have a picture of my mind as I grew up, including my early relationship with religion. I wanted you to know the psychological foundation on which my later insanity, faith and desperation was built.

I'll now change gears and show you what I more recently experienced, all the while giving you the exact sense of what I felt. Call it schizophrenia, religious experiences, psychosis or whatever you understand easiest. We're now going to have fun, and I am going to scare the shit out of you.

I'm not trying to intentionally scare (well, maybe just a little), but the extreme details of my Christian conversion and the manipulation from outside forces is too important to water down or whitewash.

God, Lucifer, damnation, salvation, Heaven and Hell, the afterlife. These all deserve some considering. Your death is going to happen and should come into your thoughts as you live. Everyone dies, both good and bad, and those in between. My story, my life, should serve as a warning for some.

I want you to take a break. Put the book down and try to imagine where it is you're going. Rest a day and look forward to what you're going to read. I want you to imagine you're in front of the looking glass about to step through. Your lips are pursed, about to drink a small potion so you can fit through an undersized door. You found the golden ticket while swallowing the red pill, and while staring into the mirror.

It took me ten years to write this book. Five years were research of psychology and theology. I couldn't write about this without a basic understanding of my mind and of God and of what actually happened to me. I spent another five years writing screenplays and short stories to hone my writing.

I don't know why I was given this opportunity, why I was taken to the other side. I do know that what I experienced, including the final outcome, follows total Biblical expectations.

If ever I do a book signing and you meet me in person, all you have to do is ask me what I honestly know and believe. I might laugh and I might even cry. But I will look you in the eye and I will tell you, what I am telling you now:

There is a God and there is a Devil. The Bible is the living word of God, and there are more antichrists living among us then you could ever believe or even truly understand.

I know what I am writing, and I accept full responsibility for it.

31

If you want to get the appropriate atmosphere for the next part of my story, I suggest you watch *Constantine* (starring Keanu Reeves) or *Jacob's Ladder* (starring Tim Robbins).

This is your optional homework if you want to fully enjoy what you're getting into. For the rest, give it a day and then come back to me. Step through the looking glass and fall down the rabbit hole, swallow the pill, and redeem your golden ticket.

STEP INTO THE ETHER WITH ME

We find ourselves in a white-tiled room. No furniture, no music, just the two of us. I look deep into your eyes and ask, "Are you ready?"

You look at me in total confusion as two chairs materialize in the middle of the room. I motion for you to sit.

As you slowly sit, end tables slowly emerge from the somewhere. They pulsate and come forth from nothing. I sit down and swoop up the drink that was on my table, bringing it to my lips and knocking it back as if it was water. You look at your end table for something next to you, something to make you feel better. It could be anything: chocolate, alcohol, cigarettes or even a teddy bear. It's what you need at this point, and you get it. It consoles you, makes you feel at ease. And it's right there.

Everything you want is there, and you grab it. I smile as we both realize that we all have our vices. I have mine right now, so why shouldn't you have yours?

I look into your eyes and stare for a moment. It's uncomfortable, but I need to make contact. I need to let you know it's okay—you might not believe everything I say, and that's all right.

"We all have choices in life," I say, "And we hear from many, many false prophets and charlatans. Sometimes we don't know where to stand, what to think or believe. But I do."

As I stand, the white-tiled room seems to fluctuate, as if breathing on its own.

I begin to pace, unsure of how to proceed, before returning to the chair.

"I'm not a prophet, and I'm not holy. I'm just a human trying to make the best of this. I make massive mistakes as well. I'm actually more of a mess then you ever could be."

You're still confused.

"You ready for the rest?" I ask. "I'll go faster now because it's needed. You know most of my early life, and the rest is just water under the bridge."

33

You shake your head yes. You expect I would be smiling, but it's more of a frown. I take another swig of my drink and lean forward to put my elbows on my knees. I continue with another necessary part—the drug part—of my history:

In ninth grade in Florida, I had my share of bullies and girlfriends, and I learned more about life. But it seemed less about living and more about survival and fitting in to get by. Mom got back with my stepfather but ended up splitting again. I learned the fun of drugs and partying during the divorce (and didn't realize the attending problems with those activities until decades later).

My sister stole things and partied same as I did, but she got caught. I was rather good at hiding my unlawful activities. Mom couldn't handle it, so she sent my sister to live with our biological father. It was probably the best thing that ever happened to her.

(My sister ended up graduating college and started a nice American life. Good job, nice house. But she was never happy. Having things, and things to do, does not make a person happy. It shows all across the world, especially in America.)

Anyway, I became a Head. That's a person who did well in school but who realized school is bullshit. Drugs and sex became a part of my life as an escape; there was nothing better to do. It was party time, and I was partying.

The white tiles begin to fluctuate, changing color as I move around in my chair. My eyes cloud over, also white.

The room flashes around you, switching from white to black to gray, then back to white again. You look around, nervously realizing that our tiled room could be a great place for some wetwork. After all, you're in a room with a madman who's been drinking, and it would be easy for him to dismember your body into little pieces. Then he would just need to take a hose and spray your remains down the drain in the right-hand corner of the room. A spigot suddenly materializes on one of the walls, and a green hose loops itself around a stake in the wall. I turn to see the hose as the spigot turns itself on.

"What are you doing?" I ask. An axe suddenly appears next to my right hand.

"I knew you would figure this out," I continue. "But not this fast." I take another sip of my drink as the axe dissolves and the hose melts onto the floor. Its liquid remnants begin flowing towards the drain.

"Stop that. I'm not your enemy, and I don't want to kill you, even if it seems like it. We are both in the ether. We're linking minds, and I'm trying to relate my experiences—not for my gain, but for yours."

A pleading look crosses your eyes, and I smile.

"This place is a gateway. It makes real our memories, our thoughts, our dreams, our nightmares come true. We're not here for your thoughts to run rampant; we're here for my memories, so keep your mind to yourself."

I finish my drink and the glass refills itself. Your drink changes color as it becomes the exact beverage you want it to be. You sip, and it's perfectly satisfying.

"Understand now?"

You nod your head and chuckle.

"Good. I'll tell you about a couple of my first times, because they were so fucked up. But they helped me realize there was something more to, say, LSD than just getting a buzz. So let's go with my first LSD experience."

The room shakes and shivers as the tiles broadcast my past:

Seventeen years old, I'm convinced to take LSD for the first time while hanging out with five high-school friends. My long hair is about five inches past my shoulders. I'm wearing a green army surplus jacket, and my jeans are methodically bleached in strips down my pant legs. I'm already stoned, and I'm being convinced by my friends to trip with them.

I took the blotter acid at David's house. David was a funny, smart friend who was always the life of the party. He had short brown hair, and he was skinny.

We walked over to John's house, right behind David's. We went to his room, because John's parents were at work. We smoked more pot in his bedroom.

The bedroom was decorated with pictures of metal bands taped to the walls. I reached over for a hit of a joint and took a big hit, holding it in.

Then, suddenly, one of the school deans bitched at me in the corner of the school's left wing. Over 300 pounds in weight, she yelled at me in front of some friends. I tried explaining to her that it wasn't my fault.

The school disappeared and I was surrounded by heavy metal posters again in John's room. My friends were staring at me.

"Dude, are you okay?"

"Yeah, why?

David laughed, and the rest of my friends chuckled and snorted.

"Dude, you starting shaking and just said, 'Ung, ung, unghhhh.'"

I laughed and told them I had suddenly found myself back at school, receiving the wrath of one of the deans.

"I'm glad you didn't meet some hot bitch wherever you went," David said. "Because that would have made us uncomfortable." We laughed more, and the joint was passed back to me.

I tripped the rest of the night with David and my friends and had one of the greatest times of my life. At the end of that get-together, I "ended up" with a ten-inch buck knife in my back pocket. And I "ended up" with some pot and a makeshift bowl (made out of a camera film case) in my front pocket. I didn't know whose they were.

In the wee hours, David said, "Dude, you have to leave. My parents can't find you here when they come back." Still tripping balls, we both guffawed, until I said, "How do I get home?"

David brought me to the garage and pulled out a bike. We laughed like hyenas because it was a bike from the 1950s with two soft tires. I was laughing because I lived ten miles away down a major highway. David must've been laughing because the bike was the shittiest one he had. It was the foggy season in Florida, and the fog that night was pure purple. Jimi Hendrix came to my mind as his song subject floated all around us. We both stared at the willowy purple swirls chasing themselves around in front of us.

I hopped on the bike, laughed some more, and clumsily fell off it as if it were a new contraption I had never ridden before. I jumped back on the bike and rode into the purple fog. I still heard David laughing for two blocks, and then I was in purple alien territory, heading for the highway.

I was still tripping as the car headlights passed and the fog swirled before me. I made it to the highway, and as each frightening car appeared suddenly then zipped past, creatures and tornados swirled out of the foggy wakes. Sometimes I was lucky enough for a cute little animal to show itself in the gloom, while other apparitions seemed intent on dragging me to Hell.

I saw faint lights ahead from a convenience store. I peddled faster and harder, feeling that my life somehow depended on arriving there. I knew what I needed, and I needed it bad.

At the store, I entered and hoped the clerk didn't realize I was out of my mind. I grabbed the biggest Charleston Chew I could find and a bag of Twizzlers and paid my $1.75 at the register without looking at the clerk's morphing face.

Back on the bike and back in the fog, I peddled my ass towards home while munching my Charleston Chew. The Chew stuck to the roof of my mouth, and the more I ate, the more got stuck up there.

A squad car passed me and made a sudden U-turn in my direction. I reached into my mouth and desperately tried to dislodge the Charleston Chew as the cop flashed his lights and pulled me over. The overweight officer approached me, and I was panicking inside. It was my first major brush with the law, and I was tripping on LSD. I momentarily forgot my predicament when I noticed the flashing blue lights were twirling magically in the fog. They made me want to chase them, but I decided against it. A voice snapped me out of it.

"How you doing, son? Late at night to be on a bike ride, huh?"

"Mumble fumble frothem home."

Oh my God! I couldn't speak intelligibly because of the damn Charleston Chew. The cop looked me over and saw inside the front pocket of my army jacket. He reached for my pot and the bowl. He grabbed it and said, "What do we have here?"

Although I knew I could only speak like a retard, I made a decision and committed to it, knowing what I was about to say was total and utter bullshit.

"I juthed cominkth from a frienths housh and I'm bikthing home."

"What about this pot?"

"The potsh and bowl—I shtole it from my sho-called friendsh becaushe I shought it wash cool. I just mooved here and became friendsh with people I shouldn't hash, but I thoughts it was cool, sho I did."

He scanned me up and down. "What's wrong with you?"

"I gotsh into a fight with shem. That's why I can't shpeak normal, because my lipsh is bushted."

He asked for my ID. I reached into my back pocket to produce it.

But I didn't just find my ID. I also found that ten-inch buck knife. I reached around it and gave him the ID. He walked to his cruiser, and my mind freaked out hard.

Here I was, looking like a drughead with my army jacket and bleached jeans, lying to a cop, talking funny because of a sticky Charleston Chew, busted for pot I barely remembered I had, tripping on acid for the first time, freaked out by swirling purple fog, and discovering a ten-inch buck knife in my back pocket.

So what does a person do in a jam like this? Obvious: Make it worse.

I reached into my back pocket and slowly eased the knife out. I had only gotten it two inches out of the pocket when the cop returned to me. Maybe I felt shielded by the swirling violet fog; I kept slowly sliding the knife out of my pocket, even as the cop started talking to me.

"You know, you don't have a record, and it looks like you moved here just recently."

My fingers kept easing the knife out behind me when I realized I could get shot dead if the cop thought I was pulling a knife on him. But I went for broke and didn't stop.

"I know what it's like to try to fit in with a new crowd, but joining them in irresponsible behavior will only get you in trouble."

The tip of the knife was almost freed from the pocket.

"You do sound like you got into a good fight."

The knife was out! I held onto it, intending to drop it. I couldn't believe I had been allowed to hold my hand out of sight all this time in the presence of a cop. I guess he didn't consider me much of a threat. If only he knew I'd been lying to his face while brandishing a deadly weapon.

"This is what I am going to do, kid."

With those words, I dropped the knife to the ground. I stepped back, onto the knife, covering it with my oversized feet. I maintained eye contact all the while, and Johnny Law didn't seem to react at all.

Instead, he took my pipe and chucked it into the woods.

"You need to be more careful about picking friends. You already got your ass beat, and it could have been worse."

He dumped my pot on the ground, shaking the baggy empty. I stepped harder on the knife. The fog's demons swirled behind him and dripped venom from their fangs. I took a deep breath and thought he actually saw the true person inside of me, wanting to believe in the innocence of youth but knowing it could be occasionally corrupted.

"You need to get on that old bike of yours and get your ass home."

He looked at me with smiling eyes, seeming to know everything I said was bullshit. I backed up, praying he didn't see the knife.

"Thanksh, I mealy appweciate this ossifer."

I rode the rest of the eight miles home like a bat out of Hell and didn't think until I was in my home. I closed my door, careful not to wake Mom. I fell on my bed and gasped, my lungs working overtime to compensate for air I didn't get while dealing with the cop.

I grabbed my Twizzlers and stared at them for the longest time. The room began to breathe as I opened my strawberry-flavored rubber and ate the most delicious, non-nutritional junk I have ever consumed. Eating those Twizzlers was like escaping from Alcatraz with a huge steak on the other side. It was one of the best feelings in my whole life.

I considered the night's events: That cop was cool; if things had gone differently, I could have gotten possession of a controlled substance, possession of drug paraphernalia, possession of a concealed weapon and, for shits and giggles, attempted murder of a police officer. Hell, he could have even pinched me for curfew violation, public intoxication, or operating a bicycle against traffic. I was lucky, but to be honest, I couldn't have talked my way out if it weren't for the Charleston Chew and the LSD. I wouldn't have been able to spin that nutty yarn if I weren't stoned, tripping and candy-mouthed. It all worked out for the best, thank God.

The tiled walls shimmy as the white bleeds through my past and becomes the present. You look at me and smile. I smile too.

OUT OF THE TV AND OUT OF MY MIND

I sit in a red leather chair across from you. I'm wearing faded jeans and a concert t-shirt, but you're not familiar with the death metal band on the shirt. My face bears a slightly graying goatee and sharp brown eyes. We both smile, and our glasses next to our chairs fill with our favorite drinks.

I slide my fingers through my slowly thinning hair and I shake the dust of life out of it. I grab my drink, lift it and let it go. It floats in the air while I rub my hands against my pants, wiping the sweat off my palms. You chuckle.

"Are you ready?" you ask.

I smile unevenly. I snatch my drink out of the air, quickly bring it to my lips but stop before I drink.

"Yeah," I say and take a sip. "Let's do this."

The nothingness takes form, and our chairs disappear. My old living room materializes around us, and we're standing in the corner. It's a one-bedroom apartment, filled with videotapes and VCRs. A nice, white-leather pit group, almost too large for the space, surrounds the small living room. The old me, er, younger me is sitting on the couch, tripping with a nitrous cracker in one hand and a punch balloon in the other. Music videos are playing on a TV in the immense white entertainment center. I'm wearing a ragged red t-shirt and a pair of ripped jeans. The room is dark except for the TV's glow. It illuminates the form of what I used to be.

You look around and notice my current self is no longer with you. But my voice breaks in over this past vision:

"Don't worry. I'm putting you alone in the situation so you can experience it with more focus. You're completely safe. Just experience it."

You watch my younger self take a nitrous cartridge out of a Whip It box and slide it into a metal something with a loud thunk. That metal something is a "cracker." You take a nitrous cartridge that is used to make whip cream and you slide it in. And then you stick the punch balloon at the other end of the metal apparatus. You twist it slowly to break the seal while the nitrous gas from the

39

cartridge quickly enters the balloon. You have to do it slowly, or you'll break the balloon from the freezing cold of the gas.

You watch me fill the balloon with the first cartridge. I twist the balloon, keep the air inside of it as I twist the cracker, and open it up while sliding the used cartridge out. I stick another cartridge into the cracker. You have questions about this, so you look up at the ceiling for me.

The sound of my voice filters all around you: "If you twist the balloon, you can put multiple cartridges into the same balloon. It makes you higher because you have more nitrous—that is, more laughing gas—in the balloon."

You turn back to the couch and watch me put three more cartridges into the balloon. I am beaming as the new Rob Zombie video comes on TV. The song is "Superbeast," and the room inexplicably dims. Zombie begins the show, as a kaleidoscope of colors and objects dance around the room. I take a hit off the balloon.

The song's rhythms rip across the room, making you agitated; the apartment becomes menacing, almost alien. You watch the TV, slowly becoming desperate to understand the growled lyrics. You decipher them a little, and you think you hear:

"Freak a leak across a ragged tongue/A dope a cross a final thing is mightily me

A cruise control, a cry out loud/The hounds of Hell are coming for me."

I take another hit. This time, I hold it in and play with the air in my lungs as I breathe in and out of the balloon. This gives an even better high.

Zombie thrashes about as the stereo speakers enlarge and fill the whole room with sound. Colors swirl around the room, dancing in front of me as I take another hit from the balloon.

"The ragged they come and the ragged they kill / You pray so hard on bloodied knees.

They ragged they come and the ragged they kill / Down into the cool air I can see."

The room gets larger and somehow smaller at the same time. Time and space become nothing as the rhythmic sounds jostle the reality around you. You watch me play with reality, or maybe reality is playing with me. It's hard for you to tell, but you lean against the wall, watching it all. Reality and fantasy collide in the hope of forming something better. The furniture twists slowly. The air shudders and breathes with a life all its own.

The balloon in my hands becomes depleted as the last of it is huffed into my lungs. I am still holding it as the character from the music video steps out of the TV, into my living room. The look on my face invites it in—hoping for something, anything beyond this reality to hold true. And it does.

The entity from the TV raises its arms, and its multi-colored dream coat spreads out before me in a psychedelic resonance of profound proportions.

40

This thing looks around me and then deep into my eyes. It is inviting me to follow it. It knows I am there for a reason, a reason that even I am only just beginning to understand. It knows I am willing to go to Hell and back to learn my purpose in life. And it knows too much about me at that moment; I feel it stare into my soul and discover what I most want in life. It is like catching a wild animal's eyes and staring deep into them, knowing you are making meaningful contact with another sentient species. Except this species is unknown, alien in its presence, or, really, omnipresence. I am looking into a supreme being's eyes and it makes me giddy with the possibility of knowledge. There is something on the other side, and I just made first contact.

I breathe out with a cascade of reality that drives it back into the TV. It closes its eyes and flows back to where it came from. Reality rushes back.

Normal.

At least, normal to the extent allowed by a four-hit acid intake. The popcorn ceiling is still waving about and things still look a little eschewed but it's really not normal. It's as a schizophrenic sees normal. Reality is a thing you see during the day while straight. Unreality is a thing that happens during drugs or very extreme events.

When you open your mind to all possibilities and to the realms of ultimate reality and you go with it, you open a door that takes you places. Each experience is a different place and each time is another truth or even a total lie. It might not be what you're looking for but it's usually something you need to know on the way to another intention. Sometimes, our mind's synapses are backfiring and all you can do is sit back and watch the fireworks until something deep within your subconscious happens. That is exactly what happened to me. The problem was, that this was my reality. And I experienced something maddening. Something that was in the fantastic had made its way through the ether and into my realm of possibilities.

I had hoped for something to shake me out of my daily reality and normalcy. And I found it. Actually, it could have found me. (But I won't pursue this line of thinking now, because that puts me ahead of myself).

The next MTV video starts, and it happens to be Kid Rock's "Bawitdaba." You see me reach for the nitrous cartridges again as I begin to fill my punch balloon up. I hope to repeat the process I just experienced.

You stop looking into my past as you're pulled back into the white room. I sit before you, smirking.

I explain that you had just seen the true beginning of my reality-altering life and my life-altering new reality. You caught me in the period when I needed something to change my life. This was just the beginning. It was a way for me to see just a little, and it was just a demonstration that true reality was not what it really is. It's more than that.

My experience proved there was something out there you can get in touch with, and it is a real as you or me. After that, I began to keep my mind open to all possibilities. Just because some people believe in an afterlife, or don't believe in ghosts, or don't believe in God ... well, that doesn't make it so.

But I needed proof. I needed my own personal belief system—not something that someone else has figured out and told me via a book, a website or a film. I needed to learn this myself. If I cannot learn it myself, then how can I fully live life? This is when I began searching for my own belief system.

VIDEO DEBAUCHERY AND THE LOSS OF THE COMIC BOOK DREAM

We both stand in my old living room, surrounded by videotapes and the same white leather furniture you saw earlier. Sitting in the left hand corner of the room is a huge desk, and it's beside another pile of tapes. You're taking it all in, especially the sheer quantity of videos that fill every available space in the room. You back up and knock over a stack of them. So I grab your arm and lead you behind my desk, out of harm's way, and sit you down in the black leather chair.

"Shhhh," I whisper. "We don't want to spook me."

Speak of the devil: We hear a flush, and I, the younger Stephen Biro, enter from the adjoining bathroom, predictably stoned. I see the toppled stack of videotapes, and even though I notice they've fallen on an order someone placed through my website, *Video Mayhem of Florida*, I shrug it off: "Fuck, I'll pick that up later." Instead, I flop down on the couch and pick my bowl up. I flick the lighter and take a hit.

I, older Stephen Biro, begin to laugh, and you look confused.

"You have no idea how many stacks of videos have fallen over!" I say. "Until now, I never could figure out why!"

I get serious:

"Do you want me here, or do you want to see my past experiences by yourself? What would be easier?"

"I want you here," you say after a moment's thought, "To explain what I need to know. But then again, sometimes I don't want you here, so I can witness it for myself."

"You're even more perceptive than I thought. Congratulations."

I continue smoking my bowl and watching TV. You look at the screen and witness a scene of a cancerous baby struggling to live in a village in the

Philippines. It cuts to a different scene, of a dead baby autopsied on a metal exam table. You wince and even gag.

"That's *Death File Black*, number four in the series," I say. "I bet you're wondering why you're surrounded by TVs and VCRs and video tapes in this small, crowded apartment?" You nod your head, wanting to hear how I got to this point in my life.

I explain that we're looking at the headquarters of my video piracy company, the business venture that immediately followed the tragic end of my comic book store. At the risk of making a short story long, I also explain to you the comic book store and its origins:

I started collecting comic books as a hobby, and I eventually began taking them to comic book conventions—buying, trading and most of all, selling. I made good money at it. As the years went on, I began managing a store in Tampa for a family company that was running a small chain of comic book stores.

I knew a pudgy, old comics seller at the flea market. I used to visit him regularly because I could fleece him of comic books that were about to explode in value. He and I became friends, and he seemed like an honest chap. Knowing he didn't have a job outside his weekend flea-market gig, I convinced the owner of the chain to hire him for another store he was just opening.

Time passed, and we both became better at our jobs, so we reasoned that the two of us should open a store together. We tried working with the chain's owners, but they were a touch too greedy. They wanted us to buy a store as a franchise. I didn't go for that.

So my new, chubby partner and I found commercial space to rent, and we put our two collections together to stock the whole store. Again, I was really good at picking the winners in the comic book industry, buying massive multiples of certain comics. They generally went up to eight to ten dollars apiece, occasionally streaking to $30. As we sat there pricing, he pulled $30 comics out of my box and three-dollar books from his. He was constantly saying, "I'm sorry," and, "Shit, that's valuable!" and, "Damn, you have thirty of those?"

I didn't care about any lopsidedness because I just wanted to have my own store with my fat ole friend. I didn't really know how to run a business, and I hoped to learn from my older partner. (I'd tell you this guy's name, but I don't want to get sued by some petty asshole. I'm still a little bitter about the whole deal, but I forgive the rat bastard. I can call him a rat bastard because it's actually a term of endearment. He understands.)

So we opened this store and most of my customers from my old chain location followed us. We kicked off a grand opening, and life was good; I was doing what I loved and it showed.

My first passion was books, but a close second was film, the more extreme the better. Since a lot of the coolest films were from overseas and didn't have stateside releases, I decided to start making bootleg copies of them and offer them for rental and sale in the comic store. My customers were in Heaven. Not only could they get comic books, Magic the Gathering Cards, or Star Wars figures, they could also watch the coolest Jet Li kung fu flicks, anime, Japanese "tentacle rape films" and every little weird foreign horror film they could never previously find. I built up one of the best collections of this stuff in the whole country.

My business partner started doing crack in the store when I wasn't there. I had friends selling him Xanax and other drugs, and he took money out of the cash register to pay them. Strangely, he was getting paranoid about *me*. I wasn't an angel either, but I wasn't doing it in the store (mainly because I didn't have to hide it from a wife and two kids). I have never done meth or the types of drugs he was using. I busted him doing everything except a prostitute in the back room.

Parents, just think about a 55-year-old fatty doing crack and selling your kids comic books. You don't want to know what goes on behind closed doors in this world.

One night, I partied hard and didn't open the store on time. I had been to a rave, partied my ass off, and ended up arriving two hours late. Mind you, I'm a slacker and had frequently opened five minutes late, ten minutes late. But never two hours before. So I arrived and found he had changed the locks. Further, he told me to fuck off, that I didn't have any ownership in the store any longer.

I went home and grabbed the yellow pages and started making calls to lawyers. I also went back into the store one evening and just walked around pricing stuff. I needed to make sure he wasn't selling our merchandise at ridiculously low prices and/or pocketing the money while not ringing it up in the register. He had taken my name off the bank account so I could no longer check at the bank. I needed to learn what the store was taking in so I could sue for a percentage of it.

I took notes on prices as the regular customers started to mutter and my jolly old red-faced business partner suggested I leave.

I refused. I made my way to the back office, and he screamed he would call the cops if I entered the employees-only area of the store. Yeah, it was another dick move on his part, but what do you expect? He's a dick.

As we waited for the police, he spun a tirade that let me know how delusional he really was. He described the exact opposite of our partnership (and, I should also say, our friendship). He told me all my comics were never mine, that I was worthless and everyone hated me at the store. I didn't help build the business up. Didn't help it run smoothly.

I listened in shock and disbelief that anyone could lie to themselves that much and not feel disgusted or ashamed. I was revolted at what this fat old man was willing to do for his own ego. I believed in fairness and honesty and thought everyone else went by those rules.

The cops came, and my soon-to-be-ex-partner said, "Officer, this man refuses to leave my store and is not allowed into the back room."

"I own half this store," I retorted. "This is my partner and we opened this store together. But for some reason, that overweight, suspender-wearing asshole changed the locks and told me to get out!"

The cop smiled and said, "This sounds like a court matter, so I suggest you both get lawyers and figure it out from there."

I was elated and certainly didn't have a bruised ego as my partner did. Understand, he was very insecure about himself. He hated that almost all the customers preferred talking to me. He had a gang of four kids that always hung around him, and he had likely talked shit about me to win their loyalty. It was his way. I tried to be personable and didn't condemn anyone for their tastes or purchases. I enjoyed every aspect of the comic book industry, and customers knew I was there for the fun and for the hobby, just as they were. It's very different than being in it for the money. But if you can earn scratch off something you love doing anyway, it's just a bonus.

He, on the other hand, made customers feel bad for having this hobby and looked down on them. A lot of patrons didn't come in while he was there. Some even sat in their cars, waiting for him to leave. It was that bad.

I can understand now why he did what he did. He was 55 years old, and a much younger guy had given him a leg up in starting a career selling collectibles. He had had a bankruptcy on his credit history, and mine was good enough to get the lease for the store. I had already had a great business, selling comics at conventions while working at the chain-store location. I had wanted to help my older friend, partly out of friendship, partly out of pity. But I thought for sure it would start a better life for both of us. I put my faith in him, and we started the store to have freedom, to be on our own schedules. To work as hard as we could to move ahead. For both or us.

I was only about 28. So it must have been painful having a hotshot younger kid doing better than you when you worked your whole life for nothing and had to start over.

My lawyer got back to me and told me I was fucked, as was my partner. If we were 49-51%, it would have been a different story, but we were 50-50 in the company, so a third party would have to come in and liquidate our business. And after everything was sold, my lawyer and my partner's lawyer would get most of the money. We would be lucky to get ten percent.

I didn't want to fuck over him and his family, even if he wanted to fuck me over. I didn't want to ruin the coolest comic book store in Tampa. I knew I could make it again on my own, and I was perfectly willing to do it. We talked, and I told him I wanted the computer, every movie, every VCR, and $2000 to move on with my life. I didn't want a single comic book even though I still

46

loved them. He brought up bullshit about deposits, so I settled for a grand. I didn't care at the time. I just wanted out so I could start life anew.

I thought about it and remembered my ex-partner once telling me he used to have a jewelry store with a partner. One day, he went to work and the whole store was cleaned out. His partner had stolen millions of dollars of jewelry and disappeared. The guy was never jailed, and my ex-partner didn't get an insurance settlement, only a bill for the last month's rent!

And here I was getting screwed over by him, after he already knew the pain of being on the receiving end. What a rotten human being (and this time, I'm not using a term of endearment).

He had me sign a non-compete clause in the dissolution contract because he was afraid of me starting a new store with our old customers. He knew I was the selling point to the business.

So with the bootleg videos, VCRs and a computer, I decided to delve into video piracy on the Internet. I really had no clue how to work the computer, and I didn't even have an e-mail address at the time. But I didn't let that stop me. The Internet was still pretty new, so I learned HTML in order to design my new-fangled website. Once the website was up, videos flew out the door.

This is where we are in my timeline now, as we gaze upon the scene in the cramped apartment. I fade away, leaving you alone with the younger me.

I sit on the couch, watching the autopsy on TV, and you hear older me's voice around you, "That's *The Basic Autopsy Procedure*. It's an actual government film from 1953, and they show it to budding pathologists before they assist in a real one."

You look in awe at the tape-covered wall directly behind you.

"Yeah, that's the collection I built up after the comic store. I traded with many other video pirates all across the world to get that library."

The collection has everything from long-out-of-print horror videos to the freakiest S&M. And when I say freakiest, I mean: scat, piss, pain, torture, mutilation, humiliation, all the way up to guys with three testicles and female amputees who sodomize guys with their stump.

I begin to ramble off more of the library. "I have Down's Syndrome kids singing and dancing in music videos, breast reduction surgery, and the uncut *Friday the 13th* which has never been released in America. I have Snow White and the Seven Dwarfs in a gangbang and all of the craziest racist Disney cartoons. I have psychedelic videos for parties and kung fu films from all over China. I even have interviews from Charles Manson and Jeffrey Dahmer that have never been released before.

"Are you ready for more titles? Here are some of the videos I was selling. I can't make this up: *The Incest Family X-Mas, Toilet Face, Pain for Pleasure, Extreme Perversions, Tard Spasm, Redneck Torture, Chicken Fucker*, and *The Golden Shower Power Hour*."

These films are even worse than you probably imagine. I was drowning in a cesspool of filth, copying trash for money and not knowing any better. I didn't have anything to do with the making of these sick videos; I just found them and made copies for people who wanted to see fucked-up shit. That's all it was: Helping people see the fucked-up shit they already wanted to see. Hell, I know I wanted to see fucked-up shit, for a while, I made a lot of money at another thing I enjoyed.

All my friends came over to say, "Steve, show me some fucked-up shit!" And I always obliged. I had it all on videotape.

You continue looking around, seeing the horror-movie posters on the walls. *Eraserhead* is behind you, and *Confessions of a Serial Killer* is in front of you. Statues and hot anime chicks in completed resin kits fill in the few spaces the videotapes didn't manage to infest. With the shelves stuffed to the gills and over flowing onto stacks on the floor, my VHS library cluttered the apartment, but it was a controlled clutter.

I say, "Look and see me for what I really was." My younger self begins to laugh hysterically.

You lean up and peek over a small order of videotapes to see me sitting on the couch, laughing at the TV. I'm watching the Stroh's Beer Wet Bikini Contest, and a chick with a double dong is fucking herself in front of 700 guys on a stage during Spring Break. She's bent over, fucking herself on stage to win whatever prize she can get, and none of the judges are stopping her. Suddenly, another contestant runs out on the stage and takes the other end of the double dong and shoves it inside her, fucking the other chick. The crowd goes wild!

You see contempt in my eyes, and you wait to hear what I have to say.

"Stupid fucking bitches! Only one of you can win the big prize, but yet both of you are on the double dong!"

I hit the stop and eject buttons on the remote control. The video pops out of the player, and I stand up.

Older me slowly fades in like a movie scene.

"Are you ready? Let's go to the next level."

YOU AND ME IN THE LIBRARY OF THE ETHER

We find ourselves in an immense, dimly lit library that smells faintly of mahogany. The walls of books are warping and twisting ever so slightly. You're sitting, staring at one of these immense shelves. The books begin dripping off them so you stare harder. You're trying to make out the names of the wiggling books before they slide down the bookcase.

I tap you on the shoulder.

"Don't even try. I've read too much in my lifetime. All of these are books I've read so far, some multiple times."

You squint, trying to make out what looks like *Huckleberry Finn* and *Fear and Loathing in Las Vegas*.

"*Fear* and *Huck* are over there." I grab your shoulder and spin you around so you can see the other wall. "You were actually looking at an amalgam of Marvel's *Infinity Gauntlet*, Clive Barker's *Damnation Game* and Homer's *Odyssey*." A silver flash shows you a contorted mirror image of the other side, behind you. You turn quickly, hoping to see what was just there when the room suddenly spins vertically instead of horizontally. You close your eyes and hope the spinning will stop when it slams like a brake, making your stomach flip.

You turn to me in bewilderment.

"I'm keeping you confused in this room so you don't have any bearings," I say.

I walk to the other chair, which turns from dark red to pitch black. I slump into it.

"The confused mind is a bit more impressionable."

You stand and walk around your chair but suddenly stop. You gaze into a fireplace you didn't notice a second ago. You don't look at me but say, "You shouldn't keep me so confused."

"Just go with it," I laugh. "Just listen to what I say and believe what I tell you. If something changes when I tell you, then take it with a pinch of salt or swallow it whole. Either way, you take breaks from this, don't you?"

You instantly think about the times you have put this book down for work, play, or sleep. Sometimes, you've stopped just to contemplate what I have been telling you.

You turn to look at me when the fireplace flames die out. The room darkens and you panic, searching around for any kind of light as the darkness envelops you. You hold your breath and try to make everything stand still as your lungs begin to scream, "Why am I not breathing?"

The darkness suddenly becomes electric as the blackness begins to dance, not only in your vision but also inside your head. You sit down in a chair you can't see and try to feel better when your stomach drops again.

You press your hands against your eyes, pushing your eyeballs inward slightly, just enough to make you dizzy. My hand grips your shoulder, easing your fear and bringing warmth to your soul for a moment.

"Don't panic; this is what I see all the time. The visions in the darkness, the static electricity of what wants to be but can't."

You let go of your breath, and it whooshes out of you.

"Breathe it in. Don't let the darkness control you. I need you to control it. Realize that you can not only control what you see in your mind, but you can change it to suit your own needs."

Imagination and reality collide inside your mind. You wince. You see some of your life flash in front of you, but you also see depraved visions of what could be Hell and see something behind it as glorious as the gate of Heaven. You twitch as the darkness moves in and out of you. It crawls up your spine and nestles in your brain like an evil thought from out of nowhere, burying itself in your psyche like a starving leech looking for a vein.

You open your eyes, not really knowing they were closed. You see me sitting on the black leather chair, smoking a cigarette. You look around as my reality swims all around you.

"Take your time. I know this isn't easy." You reach for the arms of the chair to stand when you suddenly flop into it like a puppet without a master. Your breathing is labored, and you're still bewildered. I hand you a drink, looking deep into your eyes.

"I'm sorry. I needed to give you another taste."

"Why would you—?"

I raise my hand to stop you.

"I'm about to take you into the lower levels of Hell and beyond. I need to know you're on top of your game."

You want to say something, but I cut you off again. You're in my reality now. Not yours but mine. I'm dragging you down into Heaven and Hell's laboratory, close to death with no way out until I say so. And you want to freak out over a little darkness? You want to be coddled and consoled because of your own thoughts or feelings? Do you really want to see the darkness and the evil that all men do, and do without realizing it themselves?

You gulp down the drink and set it down on the small table next to you. The table then grows and you watch your drink move away from you as your chair becomes smaller. The fire suddenly roars back to life and puts shadows across my face. My pupils expand and you see yourself in them. You don't like it, so you turn away.

I know it's hard for us to be alone with ourselves because we find the worst in us. Everyone wants to be perfect in an imperfect world but because of the human condition, we are further from that than the closest sun. Even if we are close, the little tiny things screw us up, more than we can comprehend.

I close my eyes and you do too.

You hear me say, "It's why darkness is the perfect teacher."

We are truly alone with ourselves, to forgive our soul or to forever condemn it. We can exasperate or exonerate, to curse our own life or to truly forgive it. How many times have you gone to sleep forgiving yourself or being happy? And how many times have you fallen asleep, hating yourself or accusing yourself for the things you do or even don't do? Only the true psychotic believes in themselves and has no trouble sleeping as sins pile onto sins. Knowing that sin is half the battle. Knowing your weakness is the other half of your life. No matter what you do. No matter how strong you are. You will always come short of the glory of God.

That is why I am asking you now to take a breather. I want you to put this testimony down and truly think about what you want in life. Really. I want you to think about what is important to you and what would make you happy on your deathbed. It doesn't matter if you are an atheist, agnostic, Christian, or a Buddhist.

* * *

You look me in the eyes and feel faint. You reach out to me and see the flesh of your arm oozing. Your thoughts peel backwards as your whole body contorts. Muscle and tendons rip out of your flesh and into the air with a jolt of searing pain. You're trying to scream as panic punctuates your whole being. You can barely make me out in front of you as your heart palpitates in total disbelief. I take another drink from my glass and calmly watch your body rip itself apart.

You feel your spine fuse together while your eyes pulsate, as they nearly explode from your head. The room spins, but I become the focal point in the chaos as everything erupts into something else. You keep trying to scream, flesh dripping off your face as you're painfully ripped back to your own reality.

"Be ready," I quietly say.

You dig into your skull, desperately trying to tear your own brain out, just to stop the madness. What's left of you suddenly flares into a bright light. You try to stay in my reality but realize you're not the master here.

"Get your shit together, figure out who you are and..."

By this time, you are where you are.

HALLUCINOGENIC REALITIES AND THE SHADOW
OF THE QUEST BEGINS

A circle of color swirls around you. You don't understand, but the heat of the colors put you at ease. It's as if you have given up and you're willing to let the impossible be possible. You raise your hands to watch the flesh crawl on your arms. You try to look at me as the atoms in your body begin to drift away.

Blackness envelops as the pain of another reality shifts, shifting into your reality like a death gasp from the dying. You feel yourself crossing over into death and the anesthesia of the other side. It calls you like a long-lost friend, as if it were the only place you belonged. As if…

You open your eyes with a gut-wrenching fear. You're breathing hard again. It's as if you're going to pop like a champagne cork. Covered in sweat, you panic.

I reach to you. My hand, slowly grips yours.

"You made it back I see. Good. I didn't want to wait long."

You look around. It's the same study you left. Everything is still swirling and growing, stretching and shrinking, doubling and disappearing. It's like seeing through the Mad Hatter's eyes at Alice's very Merry unBirthday. You look at me as if you've just ODed on a major psychedelic and realized it's way too much. Your stomach sinks as you clutch your face, praying a seizure isn't in the works. Your heart beats faster when you suddenly feel my strength all around you.

"It's all right. It's time."

A calm flows over you as your eyes swivel into the back of your head, obstructing your view for a moment.

Your eyes then open as you find yourself in my old leather chair, behind the desk in my old apartment. You hear my voice over the reality around you. You look desperately around at young me's belongings and take another deep breath.

(I'm sorry, gentle reader, for the theatrics I've just put you through but I'm building you up in your mind's eye. I need you to actually see where we are going to make it truly worthwhile for you. I hope you understand and can picture what is happening, because it is going, to become very visual.)

A dull pulsating flash of darkness throbs all around you. Your eyes slowly adjust. You see the younger me, hitting the nitrous while on LSD, squirming around. Looking for something to happen. You see the TV—and the stereo connected to the VCR—blaring as they pump out techno to a visual feast.

The psychedelic video on the TV is *Turbulence*. It's a hodge-podge of visual puzzles and geometric shapes that can make a psychonaut squirm with wonder while hoping for answers. The electrified geometric shapes seem to promise to unlock a portion of one's mind.

An electric buzz shoots through you as the tone dampens. The air has a metallic taste. You see me jump back as the furniture shoots up at an angle that makes the room turn. You see my body shift as the apartment twists to the opposite angle of my turn.

It suddenly morphs back to its previous state. Then it violently shifts to the left, making everything turn to the right. You see me holding away from our leaning direction when the reality in the apartment slams back to normal. You haven't had a chance to figure it out when the coffee table in front of me begins growing. It slides up itself until it's two feet higher. You marvel at this as it shifts and turns, grows and shrinks. It's not just affecting my equilibrium but my whole body, and I'm trying to hold on to the couch without falling over.

The music plays louder as the coffee table slams back to normal, as if reality didn't want to admit what it was doing.

Then a hole opens in the middle of the living room. You feel the gravity pull you towards it, and you watch me fight it with all of my strength.

I'm clutching onto the couch but the couch is edging towards the black hole, threatening to be sucked down into a stream of nothingness. The coffee table is the first to go as it melts into the darkness of the hole, which is only two feet wide. The furniture and walls melt all around me, pouring into this black hole that opened without warning.

You feel the gravity pull you too. You hold on, even though you're a shadow in this reality. You don't see anywhere to run, but you feel safe for some reason. You calm down and resume watching me. The entire apartment is in a state of flux from the unknown forces manipulating it. You don't know if it's my mind or something else, but you know something is brewing.

The apartment shifts back to normal and I flop onto the couch as if the gravity was just turned on. The black hole consumes itself, disappearing inch by inch until it's gone.

Back to normal, I smile as I take another hit of the nitrous. Lime green vines sprout and grow all around me. Plant life springs forth from the couch and the corners of the room. It crawls over the furniture in dazzling patterns only nature could make. It envelops me as the flowers bloom.

Multi-colored petals spread iridescent pollen in all directions. The smile on my face broadens into unknown territories of happiness as the vegetation continues growing around me. I pluck a purple flower from a vine wiggling in front of me. As the stem breaks from the vine, a wrenching sound can be heard as I free it from its nourishing mother. I bring the flower to my nose to smell its aphrodisiac when a burst of light emanates from all of the vines.

I quickly stuff the flower into my mouth and eat it. It slides down my throat, leaving a green organic taste in my mouth.

Then a low screech rips all around me. It is throbbing backwards in undulating screams the human mind has never encountered.

You see pain cross my face as I feel the horror of destroying something living for my own pleasure. It's as if I ate something so beautiful that life itself had to take on a whole new significance. And it did. The vines wrap themselves around me with a vengeance.

You see regret on my face. I could have smelled the flower without destroying it, but I did what humanity always does: Destroys for its own amusement without thinking. I consumed something I didn't need, not out of hunger, just a passing want.

The vines quake and suddenly dig their way under my skin, ripping flesh apart. I scream, finally realizing the truth.

You watch as two vines stretch over my head and sharpen themselves at the tips. They slam deep into my ears and bury themselves within me. My flesh peels away from the muscle as the growing vines slide under my skin. The vines grow inside of me, reaching deeper under my flesh, in every limb.

Then it suddenly stops. My flesh stops crawling as the vegetation halts.

My wounds begin to bleed as the plant life shrinks all around me. It never leaves my body, just shrinks and melts into nothingness. I've grown calm as my wounds seal and heal. Returning to normal, I breathe deeply and regain my composure.

But then my hands clutch my mouth, as I want to scream. You can tell I have realized: This is only the beginning.

I'm suddenly standing, as older me, behind the desk with you.

"You see, I think certain forces made me go through all this, trying to intimidate me into stopping my quest for God. Or maybe it was a test to see if I would continue my search for spiritual answers."

"Let's put it this way," I continue. "I think there are many markers in the search for God. Devils, Demons, Angels and even the Lord himself put realities in the way to stop us from finding out all the truth. When a person finds a certain truth, they usually stop."

What we just witnessed was the "hippie reality." I don't mean it pejoratively, but that term says everything. There was no God or the Devil. It was just earthly paradise and the magnificence of space and time. It was vegetation growing and living and showing beauty. And after being in awe of it, I destroyed it and ate of it, for my own selfish desires. Then it turned on me. The black hole was just a reminder of what we don't know that is out there.

I was looking for answers and truth, and it showed me the first beginning of truth: Nature is awe-inspiring and should be appreciated and not destroyed for personal amusement or pleasure.

This was a stepping stone in my development, but it could have also persuaded me to stop searching, by fooling me into thinking this was the entire truth.

Now examine the incident in the context of Christian iconography: Could the vines have originated from the Tree of Life, the tree God created for us to eat after we die, making us immortal? Or what if they were the Tree of Knowledge, the tree that God planted in the Garden of Eden and told Adam and Eve not to eat of, since it would give us the knowledge of life and death, of righteousness and sinfulness? I believe now that was what it was. I've learned a lot since this time, when I was practically just an animal.

Again, it was just the beginning, so I didn't know what had just happened, and I wasn't doing any research yet. Was just experiencing. Trying to find something to make sense of the life I was leading. I could believe my senses were giving me truth. Even the theory I present now is only a theory. After more of you read this, perhaps more can be explained.

In my apartment, you see the young me sit up on the couch with a huge smile on my face. I stand and spread my arms out wide and announce:

"I know you're there! It's going to take a lot more than some overgrown plant life to turn me away from finding what I need to know!"

My hand grabs your shoulder behind the desk. It's older me.

"Now we are on our way. Cabin pressure is about to exceed safety limits."

You lean back in the chair and the room fades to dark.

56

STUMBLED INTO BELIEF AND THE ASSASSINATION

I lived life like an animal at the time. But I started having experiences while on drugs that made me realize something outside my own existence was important. I didn't know its exact nature, but I could feel it. As a feeling, it built up to a point that I needed to find the answers that would give my soul rest.

If we are merely animals with a conscience, why have a conscience at all? Why feel bad doing one thing and good doing another? I didn't know, but I did know I'd already met the people who were willing to fuck anyone over for a dollar. I myself had done things to get ahead I was not proud of. I knew where my life was headed, and it felt horrible. I needed to change it.

So I was on a quest to meet my maker.

"Oh, wait, did I ever say how this atheist began to believe in God?" I ask you. "Well, I guess I should tell you."

It all happened back in that same apartment. I had recently bought a laser disc player and had it hooked up to my stereo for surround sound. I was excited. I scored a couple of hits of acid, I had some pot, and I knew my girlfriend's work schedule would give me alone time this day. I ran across the street to the laserdisc rental store next to my comic shop (this was before I fell out with my business partner). I looked for something wondrous to rent.

When I say wondrous, I mean visually intoxicating to the mind's eye. Something worthy of LSD. Something that would make my mind think beyond its rational aspect. If you can't get a picture for the type of movie I mean, let me give you some titles that are readily available:

2001: A Space Odyssey
A Clockwork Orange
Brazil
Fear and Loathing in Las Vegas
Being John Malkovich

Eternal Sunshine of the Spotless Mind
Pink Floyd's The Wall
Alice in Wonderland
Donnie Darko
Eraserhead
Frank Zappa's 200 Motels
Holy Mountain
El Topo
Naked Lunch

Most of the films listed above are visual mind fucks, and thank God they got made. Films, in a way, are much like drugs: Sometimes they are a fun escape used to forget about a shitty life or crappy job. But sometimes they can be used for mind exploring or soul searching—which was my use for drugs. And I used films to explore myself and the realms of my reality, my life and what could be my future life. Sometimes it worked and sometimes it didn't.

That's why I am telling you about the film I rented that night in the laser disc shop. After seeing it, I stopped professing my atheism, and I developed a belief in God. It caught me unawares and changed my life to the nth degree. The film is called *Final Approach*.

The hook for renting it was much less spiritual, though. I had my player hooked up to my 5.1 surround sound, and the film used all five channels, boasting 20,000 different sound effects and boasting to be the first-ever production to use all digital audio. It also promised a mind-blowing experience, and since the disc sleeve had a cool, *2001*-looking image, I picked it up. I also picked up Monty Python's *And Now for Something Completely Different*. Little did I realize that something completely different *was* in the works.

Back in my one-bedroom apartment, I dropped the discs on the coffee table and reached over to my entertainment center for my acid. It was hidden in an empty video box—one among hundreds—and if you didn't know exactly where to look, it would take you a day or two to find it.

I broke off two hits of blotter acid and stuck them under my tongue. I reached for my pot and my bowl from the same hiding spot, and I packed the bowl on the couch. I made myself comfortable and took the first hit off my pipe.

Nice and sweet—nothing too green and nothing too brown. It was just right. I laid back and let the drugs go to work. I turned on the TV and sat back even further. *Seinfeld* was on, and it was fun to watch while high. By the end of the show, I felt the acid coming on, so I slid *Final Approach* into my player.

"This is going to be good," I said to myself.

I cranked the stereo with its 5.1 surround. Back on the couch, I picked up the bowl and lighter, and it was flicked and flared before I ever realized it. The pot began to smoke.

The film's story bears repeating here because it changed my life so much. You could put this book down and find the film, watch it, then come back to this page and resume reading. Doing that would make me smile, but the movie is out of print, so good luck.

And a Spoiler Alert should be issued for anyone who might want to watch this film later. Skip a few paragraphs and pick the narrative back up after my recap.

So, with no further ado: *Final Approach* starts with a top-secret pilot flying the SR-71 Blackbird (that black plane that always makes me go "ohhh!"). He's in mid-flight when he suddenly finds himself in an office, and a secretary tells him the Doctor will see him now. Confused, he passes through the door and is met by a man standing before a huge painting. It's just a mess of blue and red that makes no sense.

The doctor says, "What do you think of my art?"

"I don't know," replies the pilot.

"I'm very proud of this because I made it myself. I like to call it 'Heaven and Hell.'"

With art talk out of the way, they sit across from each other and begin a session. The pilot goes through a battery of mental tests, as he seems to have amnesia. The pilot gets flashes of his life and top-secret Air Force work, but it's still a jumble to him. He sees one wife after another, and his flashes of memory make little sense to him, but he carries on.

Then the doctor tries something new. They sit on a different set of chairs, with a small coffee table between them. The doctor asks, "Do you want an apple?"

The pilot looks at the small tray of apples and says, "No."

"Okay," says the doctor. "I need to really talk to you, and I want the most honest answer I can get." The pilot is game.

"Do you believe in God?" asks the doctor.

The pilot freaks out in his mind. You hear all his thoughts as he tries to determine if he is captured by the enemy, has been thrown in a parallel dimension, or is just having a dream. He looks at the doctor and answers, "No!"

He stands and almost threatens the doctor while screaming that he doesn't believe in God. It becomes the most intense part of the film, as the viewer knows what is happening and I'm screaming at the pilot to stop! But he doesn't.

The doctor stands and lays his hand on him and says, "Well, this is about life!"

The pilot suddenly finds himself in his last living moment. He has died while on his last mission and realizes he just cussed out God and told him he doesn't believe.

This scenario was a ruse to discover who he was as a person; God took the time to talk and analyze him before sending him to where he belonged.

(Spoiler Alert ended!)

I was in the moment and I believed. Actors James Sikking (the pilot) and Hector Elizondo (the doctor) are perfect in the film. The tragedy that occurred is damnation because the pilot never thought about it.

I realized I had never really thought about God or the afterlife as I merrily went towards one or the other. I had basically been in that pilot's shoes, telling God I didn't believe in him, and for such a stupid reason as not taking time to really think about it. It blew me away.

I hadn't counted on this movie questioning everything about my beliefs. But it did. I began thinking about my whole life, thinking about what I would say to God if face to face with Him. I had told plenty of people I was an atheist, simply because I never thought about it, because my Dad's belief influenced me, and because of a few problems I had in early church experiences.

I took a look around the apartment, looking at every item intensely. I noticed a divine pattern in everything. All the marvels around me came into focus, and I saw how I had taken them for granted. I saw the beauty of how we controlled electricity, using it for our own needs. The TV, stereo and computer suddenly became sources of amazement to me. I saw plastics and wood, fabric and metal twisted to shapes for our use. I opened the front door, gasping in awe at the logical progression of everything in the world, working together for everything and anything we needed.

I began to realize how perfect aspects of this world really are, and I was Godstruck. I returned to the couch, leaving the front door open to circulate fresh air in the apartment. I sat and prayed to God for the first time in my life. I told him how sorry I was for not noticing His work.

After that night … "I believed in a God."

But that's all it was, and that's exactly what I gave Him, just a belief in Him. Not the Holy Bible God yet. I only knew there was a Creator and that He loved me and I loved Him. There was no Hell as long as I believed in Him.

That's what the movie had shown me and that was exactly what I had needed. I didn't realize it was just another marker on the path to greater wisdom. How could I know that it was actually the beginning of my path to the Netherworld? I hadn't realized a belief in Him necessitated a lifestyle change. I just thought a belief in God saved you; that was all. After seeing that film, I pictured myself in front of God, telling him I believed, and not being in trouble for the other choices in my life. So I continued my life of depravity.

We're back in my apartment again:

My happy ass sat on the couch, watching the movie *Fight Club* on TV. My eyes were pure black as the acid reacted to my pupils. The movie was at the point where Tyler Durden grabs a Vietnamese clerk and drags him from the store, into the back alley.

I knew something was going to happen as I took a hit off of a nitrous balloon. The room began flowing and then took on the features of a parade.

60

Everyone was dressed in late '50s or early '60s clothing. A 1961 Lincoln Continental drove down a road, surrounded by a procession of police and others. Two people were waving at and greeting everyone they passed but didn't slow down.

In the back of my mind, I knew the identity of the waving Lincoln passenger, and I jumped off my picnic blanket and raced towards the vehicle.

"I have to save him! I have to!" I yelled.

I made a running leap towards President John F. Kennedy just as a loud crack broke through the air! I felt my head slowly explode in a spray of blood and brains. My thought processes instantly clicked off. No sooner did my body hit the ground than I materialized back on my couch. I was breathing hard.

I didn't understand what happened but I still felt it.

"What the hell was that?"

I paced around the living room, simultaneously confused and exhilarated. I couldn't shake it off. I knew Kennedy was supposed to die, but I found myself in the position to help him and I did, without thinking, without worry for my own life. That's when I realized I would die for a greater good. Not just for my country but for any country and any family and any person.

I looked up from the couch and saw *Fight Club* still playing. Ed Norton was about to shoot himself in the face to get rid of his false self, his Tyler Durden self, and he did. That is where I was at, more or less.

I was pretty shaken by what had just happened. I slipped on my jean jacket as I walked outside to get some fresh air. The cool night air helped me think. I came to an understanding that my drug use was no longer just an escape. I was beginning to learn things about myself and my life.

It was as if I tapped into the hidden knowledge of life. I became giddy on finding the road less traveled. I found the philosopher's stone that had been ballyhooed for ages. Secret wisdom was now at my fingertips every time I mixed LSD with nitrous, because I always walked away with a better understanding of my life than before. Each time, I was transported to another level of existence. I'd done acid hundreds of times before but had never mixed it with nitrous. I had also never been transported to someplace different nor had out-of-body experiences.

I began to get smarter about what I was doing. I became a technological shaman. The earlier shamans were using the natural guide of magic mushrooms or pot to experience deep trances and help their tribes with new wisdoms. I was mixing the technology of our society with the chemistry of modern man to explore the recesses of my reality and my mind.

At this time, I believed I found the actual philosopher's stone: The mix of N20 and LSD-25 in the human body, 400 to 800 micrograms of LSD and 12 to 16 Whip It cartridges filled in three to four punch balloons. This would give you five to seven minutes with the philosopher's stone. I used big black paperclips to hold the other punch balloons closed while going on my journeys into the ether.

So I found that extreme amounts of both drugs brought about hidden wisdom and secret knowledge. From that point forward, I began my quest to find secrets men have never known. Or to come to grips with truths that have been discussed for ages but to actually experience them firsthand instead of reading them in a book. I was going to the other side.

MORPHEUS STEPS OUT, PAST LIFE REGRESSION STEPS IN AND THE QUEST TO FIND GOD MATURES

I was back in my living room, and *The Matrix* played on the TV. I got comfortable on the couch, waiting. Then I sat up abruptly, thinking the movie had some kind of instructions for me. But it didn't after all, and I lay back down.

I took a couple of hits off the nitrous and let the buzz overtake me. When the drug wore off, I took a couple more hits one after another. I played with it, holding each breath as if it were my last. Three more balloons, filled up, sitting next to me on the couch. I blew my carbon dioxide and N2O mix back into the balloon and then took another hit. The room felt fuzzy.

Then it happened.

Morpheus walked into the living room, and the room suddenly flashed away, just like in the movie, and the apartment became pure white. He sat down in the love seat next to me. He wore the same type of clothes from the film, but he looked out of place on my leather love seat. He didn't call me Neo and didn't tell me about the Matrix.

Instead, he asked me, "Are you willing to find out the truth?"

I didn't question anything and just went with it.

"I want the truth no matter what."

"Good!" he said, smiling.

I sat there and looked at Morpheus, er, Laurence Fishburne. (Nah, let's go with Morpheus. It sounds more ominous, which is fitting.)

We stared at each other for moment, and I could see deep into his pupils. I could make out what looked like galaxies swirling around in his eyes. A shiver ran down my spine as I realized he was the entity that I'd met before, the one that had seemingly stepped out of the Rob Zombie video.

Being in the presence of something from the other side was truly harrowing. I averted my eyes, looking down at the white floor. I squeezed the leather of the chair to make sure it was real.

"This isn't Kansas anymore." I said out loud.

Then...

I find myself as a World War II pilot flying for the British RAF. I jump into the seat of a plane as the mechanics pull away the stops to let the wheels roll free. Sirens blare in the background, and people were running all around. I rev the plane's motor and turn the aircraft towards the runway.

I look up as 25 German fighters turn down out of the sky, towards the base. Bullets rain down on several of the other planes on the runway as I get into take-off position.

(This was my body. I was like a fly on the wall, except what the fly was watching was *himself*. I didn't, and don't, know how to fly, but I've seen them in documentaries about World War II.)

I pull my plane into position and speed it down the runway. My hands and feet work the controls properly, to my amazement. The plane arches up into the atmosphere, and it basically does what my body commands. Other planes follow behind me.

I pull on a lever, and the plane screeches into the air as the city below me shrinks. Looking down at the city, I see it's devastated.

From the side, I see German planes flying towards us. I turn the plane to face them, only to find another enemy plane behind me.

The bullets pierce the plane as I hastily try to turn. It doesn't work, and my engine explodes in a rain of fire and fuel. The plane lurches to the right, then towards the ground. The gas in the cockpit flares. The mechanics of the plane are failing as I try to pull up. I'm on fire while going down like a ton of bricks.

My ejection seat doesn't work, and I pray to God. The earth spins towards me, and I plummet increasingly faster towards the devastated city below. I hit it with an explosion that jars me past death.

Then...

I was thrust back into the leather chair across from Morpheus. I was sweating, confused, and the smell of burning hair and flesh covered my clothes. I breathed deeply and sat up, and I looked at the entity. He smiled and glanced down towards my chin, likely so I wouldn't look into him anymore.

"Let's finish this," he said.

The whiteness of the room lurched backwards. It swished and flowed as reality began to shape itself into what it needed to be. Then...

I suddenly find myself as a Zulu tribesman. I'm amidst a thousand other warriors listening to the chief of the tribe, and we scream the answers to his calls. I'm just part of the masses and enjoying the life I am leading with the friends and family that surround me.

I step back and find myself in my village. It's the village of my birth. People greet me, knowing me from childhood, and they respect me.

A wave of time exerts itself, and I find myself on the plains of Africa. I have a spear in my hand and I am chasing an injured gazelle. I run as fast as I can until I trip over a vine. My prey continues to run away as I pull myself up, brushing off the dirt. I look around.

(Here I was again, in another body, and it felt very natural. I stopped and looked at my hands and was just amazed. I couldn't believe I was African. I couldn't believe I was black! What the hell is going on?)

I hear a rustling in the grass, to my left, and I crouch down quickly. My hand reaches for my dropped spear. Then the tall grass to my right begins rustling, and the crunching of the dry grass on my left gets closer. A lion's tail sways in the air about ten feet away from me.

I'm faced with three female lionesses moving in for the kill.

"Big kitties," I foolishly say aloud.

(This was me saying it, not the body I inhabited, but little ol' me. I could suddenly picture several of my pet cats getting ready to play with me, except I was 600 pounds smaller than the cats. It dawned on me to run!)

I run so quickly I astonish myself. (And before you say it, it's not because I was black, it was because I have never had three female lions want to eat me before!)

So I run and I run and I run some more. I've only run about 50 meters when the first female lion tackles me. I can feel the claws dig into me at multiple angles. They either go deep or begin to shred. The smell of the cat is musky, too musky, as I grab a lungful of air. My lungs are expanding while spasms shake my body. Her teeth bite into the lower end of my spine but it doesn't paralyze me. She must have been younger than most to not be giving me the deathblow.

Another female lion bites into my leg, her jaws clamping down while slowly snapping upwards. Gnawing. Her teeth scrape my thighbone, and I finally have enough time to scream. The pain washes through me, and I feel numb. Pain and numbness are almost impossible to describe when they happen at the same time.

A third lion approaches my face. It stops with paws on either side of my head. I can only see its broad, matted neck when she looks down, while opening her mouth. Her jaws wrap around my skull, and she bites down hard. The pressure begins to build when her fangs pierce the bone and drive home.

Then...

I abruptly found myself on my couch again.

"What the hell was that?" I asked.

My body was on edge, but I was emotionally calm. My physical self had reacted from dying twice in a row, but my mind had already come to grips with it. It's hard to explain. I was elated while freaked out.

I looked for Morpheus, but the bastard wasn't there.

I grabbed my cigarettes and decided to take a walk around the apartment building. I wanted to figure out what had just happened. I began to theorize to myself:

"Okay, we have the same entity I met before. This time it was in the shape of Morpheus from *The Matrix* or perhaps just Laurence Fishburne, who played Morpheus in *The Matrix*."

Somehow the movie I was watching became real, or more likely, the character I was watching was hijacked by something else, using that form because of its familiarity to me, or because it was currently in my experience, and it needed an empty host to fill in order to show me things.

I experienced a part of the movie, but it was different. Last time, it was in the form of Rob Zombie, because I was watching one of his music videos. It used the forms of what I was watching on the TV, so maybe it needs that— images I already have in my head—to make contact.

I continued my cigarette while walking in circles in the apartment complex.

"What was it that I just experienced?" I asked myself. "Was it reincarnation? That must have been reincarnation. But why would I experience that? Why did I just experience two different lives and then death so fast? I don't believe in reincarnation. Never thought about it. Whenever someone brought it up, I couldn't listen to them, I always thought it was pure silliness. But on the other hand, I just had a crash course in alternate lives."

"What the Hell was Morpheus doing talking to me about truth? When the Hell did a hallucination ever really interact with me to this extent?"

I saw a nice big tree to the left. It was about 4 a.m., but nobody lived near this tree. I plunked my ass down against it, reached for another cigarette, and put my thoughts through a mental checklist.

I knew, no matter how intense the experience, what I felt might not be the truth. But I knew something was there, talking to me. I found myself in either past lives or being reincarnated twice. It wasn't really me, but I was somehow there experiencing it.

Then again, maybe it was me. And was it God showing me this? Or was it something else? I tended to think though, that what I experienced was false. I mean a World War II fighter pilot and an African tribesman, both having thrilling adventures. How come I didn't have boring moments in past lives? You never hear anyone say they know their past lives and they were boring.

Was that the truth? We all reincarnate, and there is neither Heaven nor Hell? The Hindus believe a person can reincarnate up to seven times. They also believe in reincarnating as a bug.

Seven is a holy number. I only experienced two, and this "Stephen Biro" life makes my third. What if I only have seven? Then I have four more to go, unless I was only shown two and not the rest. What happens when you get to seven? Is that when you go to Heaven or Hell? Did I already live seven lives and this is Hell? Was that God masquerading as Morpheus so my mind can wrap around it? Was he an angel? Shit, what if he was a demon? Couldn't be a demon, because I was taught about reincarnation and other life lessons. What if it's another marker or level meant to seem like an answer so searchers stop looking for God? It could be another personal truth that prevents me from persisting towards the ultimate truth.

I've talked about the markers before, the ones that people reach and then either stop, turn around or keep going beyond. This wasn't my marker. This wasn't my reality. Maybe it is for Shirley MacLaine and the millions who believe in reincarnation, but it wasn't mine. It would be too simple.

Reincarnation has no bearing on my life. If it did happen before, if I did live those lives, well, cool. But that's not what I was looking for. I know there is a Creator, and I want a true understanding. I refuse to be let off at a different stop when the train goes all the way to the end.

I have endured mind fucks of physical destruction, but it wasn't actually harming me physically.

But then I quickly remembered getting killed by lions, crashing an airplane, being ripped apart by the Tree of Life and almost getting sucked into a black hole.

Yes, I was still alive and unharmed but it's just like every experience you have in your everyday life: You will always carry a memory of it, so these things may be damaging my psyche.

But I didn't care. I could live with it.

At that time, it was plain to me: If you believe in God and trust Him, He would answer you. God answered many men and women before, and just because nobody claims meeting him recently doesn't mean he won't say, "Hello."

Every civilization has its beliefs and mystic encounters with their gods or God, angels or demons. Some societies used peyote or mushrooms, and I'm sure some of them had ergot poisoning as well.

So I began to wonder: What if I killed myself doing what I was doing? Could I be sent to Hell, for dying while searching for God this way?

I decided no.

I knew in my heart that if I put myself in spiritual or physical danger, God would step in. I've gone to different places with my mind because of drugs. But I didn't create drugs or their interaction with my brain. God did.

If God created drugs, mushrooms, cocoa leaf, poppy plants and marijuana, who am I to say this is not how He intended for us to contact Him? All I knew at the time was that LSD and mushrooms opened my mind to new thoughts. It is one of only two chemicals that produce the same results and that interact and fall into a specific spot in the serotonin receptors. It's the two drugs that create an actual trip that doesn't kill you.

Nitrous intensifies the effects one thousand fold. Not everyone knows this, because it is a rare person who goes to the dentist for a tooth drilling while tripping on LSD or mushrooms!

I began to take notes of what I was experiencing at this time. I knew what I was experiencing was not normal, so after each vision, I wrote on my computer exactly what I went through. I figured it would be helpful as the years progressed and the memories faded. I would have a diary of each hellish delight and every heavenly pursuit.

Maybe someone would want to read it because they needed answers too? Maybe what I was trying to do was almost impossible to do in this day and age. Most people can't take a year off from reality to find God and truths for themselves.

So maybe, just maybe I was doing something important. Maybe my life would mean something after I was dead and buried. Maybe... (Okay, I'm saying "maybe" too often!)

But hopefully, my time on this plane of existence will allow others to open the same door I passed through without having to do all the groundwork. They won't have to build their own door because I left breadcrumbs to mine. They won't have to find a key, because I made a copy. Writing out the experiences made my quest take on an even bigger purpose. I knew I would either find God or die trying.

THE RESURRECTION CHAIR, SCHIZOPHRENIA AND THE FUTURE SELF

The next weekend, I decided to do the same thing: Watch a couple of psychedelic videos and end with *The Matrix*.

As the drugs took hold, the video cascaded all around my apartment. A flash enveloped me and then...

I find myself in a chair in an immense futuristic auditorium. I am looking up at a huge concave screen in front of me. I notice my hands and legs are strapped to the chair. The straps aren't too tight; they feel comfortable. I look around as far as my neck can stretch and see only darkness. But I hear shuffling noises behind me.

Then the screen catches my eye with something shocking:

There I am, on the enormous screen. I'm living my life normally, working out of the apartment, hanging with friends, having a good time.

As I sit watching my life, I notice a metallic ring around my head that pulsates with a bluish hue. It's almost like a halo, and it's attached to the chair.

I look back at the screen and watch myself sitting on the couch, taking acid and getting ready to do a couple of balloons of nitrous.

"You have to find the answers," I yell at the screen. "Don't stop until you find the answers!"

Behind me, I hear boos and catcalls. I crane my neck and can now see countless shapes, as if people are sitting in chairs behind me. I can hear soft murmurs of what they are saying:

"He's becoming self-aware."

"Why is he ruining his life for us?"

"He better not screw this up. It was getting interesting."

"When is it my turn to sit in the resurrection chair?"

"He's not supposed to wake up while in the chair."

"No one ever has except for Him."

"No, there have been others."

A humming emanates from the chair. It becomes louder and louder as the seconds progress. I grit my teeth under a sudden intensity. Blackness envelopes me.

Then...

I found myself sitting on my couch in the living room again. I place my head in my hands and let out a huge sigh because I knew what I had to do.

I started searching the messy apartment for the video cameras. I searched every corner, every cabinet. I got a screwdriver and pulled a chair over to the air conditioning vent. I undid the screws, popped the vent off and stuck my hand inside, almost certain I would pull out a camera.

I pulled out a handful of dust bunnies instead. On my tiptoes, I peered inside the vent but saw no camera.

I flopped down on the couch and thought. Where was I? Was that Heaven? Was God in the audience? It sounded as if people were watching my life for their own amusement. Was that chair a way for souls to relive life and give people entertainment at the same time? So if that was another reality, what did it mean?

I continued looking around for cameras when I spied a fly in a corner of the ceiling. Then I thought: What if God used the eyes of everything as if they were cameras? Every insect, every animal and every human might be God's eyes! If He did it this way, God could see everything everyone was doing by every perspective. Animals were everywhere, from the microscopic to the family dog. With that thought, I looked over to my dog, Mr. Biscuits.

I rescued Mr. Biscuits from the humane shelter about a year ago. He was a mutt but the best mutt a man could have. I called him over because he was sitting in front of the TV. He jumped onto the couch, next to me. I reached over and took his snout, looking him in the eyes.

"Testing... 1 2 3," I said. I laughed, wondering if this is what schizophrenia was like. "Can you see me?"

My dog pulled away and then gave me the biggest smile I have ever seen on an animal. His lips pulled back to resemble a giant, cheesy human grin.

"Did you just smile at me?"

Mr. Biscuits jumped off the couch and ran for his stick that was lying on the carpet. He picked it up with his teeth and pranced to the door. He turned around and looked right at me, still smiling.

I guess God's organic security camera wanted to play fetch. So we played fetch. In the darkness of night, I threw that stick until my dog was tired and thirsty. We had a great time together, but all the while, I wondered if I had lost my mind completely. Or was God actually using other's eyes to see this world? And did God actually make my dog give that cheesy-ass smile as a cosmic goof because I discovered another universal secret? Or was I just slowly going insane?

It was time for another round, time to open myself up to more possibilities. If I went nuts and lost my mind, so be it. I dropped more acid and got the balloons ready for another excursion into the netherworld.

I popped in another videotape of more psychedelics and turned up the stereo. My dog rested beside me and went to sleep. I picked up one of the balloons and began pulling off the sweet nitrous oxide inside.

Then....

I find myself in a great hall. I'm much older, about 58. My hair is grey and thin. I wear the clothes of a priest. I hear thousands of people, waiting for me to take the stage.

A very small dwarf walks up to me. He also wears the clothes of a priest.

"Stephen, they're ready," he says.

A sultry woman walks up to me. Her long hair is dark in the dim light. She wears long black boots and a black skirt. She also wears a black-and-white striped corset. Her arms wrap around me.

"It's time, lover."

She kisses me deep as another person walks up.

"Stephen, we have all the gates closed, and security is on the watch for anything out of the ordinary. We don't want a repeat of last time."

"Thanks, Jacob," I say. "It means a lot to me."

Jacob turns and walks away. He wears a tactical military uniform but with bits of flair on it that makes me look at him questionably. I notice several patches for The Misfits and The Cramps on the back of his bulletproof jacket. I also see a tattoo that climbs up his neck like a jagged lightning bolt.

(It was the same pseudo-out-of-body feeling I had with my past lives except this was in the future. I didn't fight it; I just let the body do its work while I sat there, nestled in my brain and enjoying the ride.)

Techno music plays as I stride onstage, in front of 20,000 people. The music goes up and down as if on a rollercoaster, and the crowd goes wild. There can be no way these people are all here for me, I think. I look into the crowd and notice a pattern: I could see the people are in revolt against what America had become (and what the world had too). As I scanned the faces, I see joy in their hearts but death in their souls. I see every single soul and what it wants to be, while seeing how torn and diseased it is from living on this planet. My mind begins to choke.

I see several people hitting nitrous out of small-pressurized guns. I also see balloons in the distance, floating around. People hit off them too.

"What the hell became of me?" is all I can think.

I walk to the microphone stand and remove the mic. People suddenly stop moving. The techno music stops, and I notice a band behind me. They begin to play. It's a heavy sound but not too overbearing. I lift the microphone to my lips and just hold it there. I see huge screens to my left and right, and I see

71

monitors below me. They display scenes from other halls and other stadiums around the world.

I'm nervous, but the onstage Stephen isn't. He's ready to spit fire and brimstone. The metal music goes to a steady, slow rhythm as the words flow from me.

"Welcome my children. I welcome you with open arms and an open heart."

The crowd chants back, "And we welcome you!'

"Today is the day! It's July fourteenth, two thousand and twenty one! It's Seven, fourteen, twenty-one. Seven plus fourteen equals twenty-one. Or how about twenty-one minus seven equals fourteen. Now, fourteen minus seven is seven. And take July, which is the seventh month, times it by the beginning number of the century and you get fourteen. Seven plus fourteen is twenty-one! Three sevens! You look at it: It's divisible, it's subtract-able, it's added and it's multiplied. Backwards or forwards, either way you look at it, seven is the holy number of the Lord, and three sevens is the ultimate number of God, while three sixes is the number of the beast."

Everyone boos until I raise my hands for silence. The metal music picks up in tempo as my rant continues.

"The beast has had his day. This country was founded on Mammon! The people of this land were originally killed because of greed. Capitalism is just another name for greed. We have been fooling the rest of the world by saying freedom and capitalism will make this world a better place, pushing these tracts of our government's founding principles."

(I was bewildered at the intensity and the throngs of people as I sat behind the eyeballs of myself.)

"Most of us live on the street or in houses we don't own. Wall Street gave then it took. The government gave, and then they took it back for the greedy and brought the ruin of America and the industrialized nations to its knees. All the countries with cheap labor used by the greedy were tapped out at the point that each country's citizen was almost at the point of living decently, so the greedy took their corporations and jobs to the next impoverished country. In their wake, they left the hungry, the needy. They left the dreams of a better life, smashed, rolled over with a steam roller. And the first country that capitalism destroyed, was its own."

I pace the stage as the music and lights reach a fever pitch.

"Every one of you has been looked down on because of your beliefs, because you followed me as I follow Him! We all believe in our Lord! We all want a personal friendship with the Lord and not just an imaginary one. We all want to worship the Lord in the way that we found in our hearts and not behind a wall of brick and stone."

The crowd goes insane with jubilation as my pacing becomes more frantic.

"We had put up with going against the word of God for so long that we are beaten down. We have been led to the slaughter by the god of corruption and greed, and we will not take it any longer!"

The congregation applauds and screams hallelujahs!

"This world is sick of the misery and devastation of the greed of man! We will take it back! We will destroy the worshippers of the golden calf! We will smite those who gave their souls to the Devil. We will find those who destroy this world while trying to steal our salvation by forcing us to worship the gods of their own making! They're leaving us with sickness and death because it was in the fine print of a contract from the Devil we never signed and we certainly have never seen!"

I begin to cry on stage, and the crowd becomes silent.

"There is enough food and medical supplies in this world to heal and feed everyone of this planet. The Lord gave us this planet to take care of all people, not just some of us."

I wipe tears from my eyes as the music becomes more ominous in tone.

"The vengeful Lord smote his enemies! The Lord said he would one day visit the Israelite's sins upon them. For worshipping the golden calf while Moses was in communion with God!"

The music gets heavier. The crowd gets restless.

"God's green earth can no longer sustain itself for those who worship the golden calf. Those who have put this planet in jeopardy shall no longer live. We have been working hard for this day to come, and we have help from every God-fearing being on this planet. Many will say they believe, when in their hearts, they truly worship Mammon."

I feel pain and frustration in heart and soul. The world's devastation and destitution feels like a death surrounding everyone.

"Pay attention to the marks on the doors and the buildings of those to be saved. Spare the children unless their names are marked in the Book of Black. Admonish those in the Book of Sleep and heal those in the Book of Life."

"Not an innocent soul, not a one, will be harmed tonight. But a corrupt soul will be used to wake those who sleep, and the streets will run red with the blood of the worshippers of the calf!"

I bow my head as the music suddenly stops.

"May the Lord God forgive us for it is now, finally, war. The soldiers of misfortune have overtaken the God-fearing people of this world. We have been killed and left to die over greed. We cannot survive this world, for soon, the damned will be left alone on this planet. And when the damned breed, future innocent souls will be born into this world of the dead. We go out tonight to take back the world for the innocents of the earth and for the future souls you create, Lord."

73

"Please forgive us! Please give us the strength to accomplish the salvation of the world! We only do this to save those in need! The Meek ... shall now ... inherit the earth!"

I begin to scream it.

"The Meek shall now inherit the earth! The Meek shall now inherit the earth!"

All over the world, people chant the words, over and over again.

"THE MEEK SHALL NOW INHERIT THE EARTH!"

"THE MEEK SHALL NOW INHERIT THE EARTH!"

I fall to my knees as the people leave the stadium, chanting. I pray The Lord's Prayer, words that will forever echo in my mind.

"Our Father, who art in Heaven..."

MORPHEUS RETURNS AND THE SPLITTING OF THE EGO

I sat on my couch, dazed and a little confused. I opened my eyes and noticed Morpheus sitting on the love seat right next to me. I was still groggy from my onstage appearance and full of questions. Morpheus wasn't wearing his leather getup from the movies but rather a nice grey suit and dark sunglasses. I leaned over and put the empty balloon down on the coffee table.

"What's with the sunglasses?"

"You already know the answer," he chuckled.

"I want to hear it from you."

"I don't want you to look into my eyes anymore."

I picked up a pack of Marlboros and slid one out.

"Do you want one?" I asked.

"No, you go right ahead."

I lit the cigarette and took a hearty pull off it.

"You shouldn't smoke. It's bad for the soul," he said. He then stood and paced a little. "Don't you have some questions for me?"

"Yes. Are you God?" I asked.

"I'm not allowed to answer that."

"Why, is it written, or is it something God doesn't want you to say?"

"Nice try, but I can't say."

He walked back to the love seat and sat.

"You're a mystery to us, Stephen Biro. We know what you're trying to do, and we know that you're actually doing it. Better men have come this way, the road less traveled, and they usually give up. Usually the physical side effects make them stop. But not you."

I lifted my hand and watched it tremble, like Parkinson's disease. I shook it off and said, "I don't care about my body or my health. I know what will make me die happy, and that's to know and find God."

75

"You've been close to death many times. I could even say that you have died but then I would be wrong, strictly speaking. Let's say a part of you has died and you're wanting to—no, needing to— replace it."

"So what is going on and why haven't—?"

"You are going through what most people on this planet would kill for. You're coming across ideas and realities that some of the greatest men in history have experienced. So far, you have experienced what certain religions have based their complete teachings on. It's not good enough for you."

"You're right," I said. "I'm looking for true reality and for what I am really up against."

"So, you're 'up against' something? Are you saying you have an enemy? Are you saying God is your enemy?"

"I never said that. Let me say it in a different way: I need to know the score and the actual rules of the game, not just here on earth but beyond this reality. Beyond what my five senses can understand. I need to know the real game behind all of this."

Disappointingly, Morpheus then quoted Morpheus, "What if I gave you the opportunity to know everything that you wanted to know but your life would forever be changed and you may never come back."

"I'd say, 'This isn't the movie and I'm not Neo.'"

"But it is the same quest, no? Neo's quest in the film has been a pursuit for men for as long as they have been alive. If it helps, you can close your eyes."

"I prefer the visual."

He reached into his jacket and produced two pills: One red and the other— you guessed it—blue.

"You take the blue pill," he said, "And the story ends. You wake up in your bed and believe whatever you want to believe. You take the red pill and you stay in Wonderland and I show you how deep the rabbit-hole goes."

"You can't rip straight dialogue from the Matrix!" I laughed. "You could have done something different!"

Morpheus just continued to hold his hand out for me to pick.

My mind began racing. I wasn't on Nitrous so something was different here. This wasn't the fucking Matrix. This was my reality, trying to find God. The movie had nothing to do with God, so let's start with that.

I had a choice: red or blue. Blue has always signified Heaven, and red has always signified Hell. Even in *Final Approach*, it was a blue Heaven and red Hell. So the blue pill was the one I should take. I believed in God, but this entity in the guise of Morpheus (or really more of Laurence Fishburne when he's out of the leather costume) could have been fucking with my head. Or could he really have been offering the truth—but in the red pill? Red is chaos, fire and lust all wrapped up in one beautiful color. Blue is peaceful, tranquil and has a loving feeling if it's in the right hue.

I reached out and picked the blue pill.

76

"Why did you do that?" he asked.

"Because this isn't the movie. Wisdom, knowledge and peace are always calm, always serene. Blue has never been a color that warns, tells you to stop or signifies danger. Red does."

"You're even more of a mystery than we thought, Mr. Biro. You've made your choice; let's hope it's the right one for your sake."

He slowly dissipated, leaving a trail of electrified particles in his wake. I reached for my cigarette in the ashtray and lit it, taking a couple drags. Then I reached for the cracker and slipped another cartridge into it. As I reached for the balloon, I noticed the TV had been playing static the whole time.

"That isn't what I expected."

Actually, I didn't know what to expect since I turned down the entity's offer. It offered me the truth—but whose truth? It wasn't just a hallucination either. Not for that long. I couldn't even be certain it was the same thing I had met before. I couldn't see its eyes, probably because it didn't want me to see whether it was the same entity or not. It didn't want me to look inside it. I became confused about everything.

I took a hit off of the balloon and held it in.

Maybe the different things I experienced were stored in the DNA of every person? Or maybe I was coming across old thoughts that still circulated across our world long after the thinker had passed. If our bodies are alive because of electricity in our mind, and if our thoughts were minute electrical sparks that jumped between synapses, maybe those sparks not only finished the thought in our minds but went beyond the mind!

Maybe energy floats all around us that are leftover ideas and thoughts of people who earlier lived on this earth. Maybe this energy sometimes connects with our own mind's synapses, turning our thoughts into theirs?

Or maybe I was just schizophrenic and totally insane. I took another hit off of the nitrous balloon. I held it in and then blew out the gas.

I didn't fucking know, but I kept doing this because it felt like progress. Even if I was fucking out of my mind, it made sense to me.

My head became warm. I felt that I could be aware of every thought and every electrical discharge zipping around in my brain. Shivers ran down my spine and the hairs on my head tried to stand straight up. A dull throbbing rippled through my skull. I clutched the sides of my head as the throbbing became a pulse. It was a heartbeat rhythm but it quickly turned excruciatingly painful, and it felt like as if my brain was tearing apart.

It fucking was! It was wrenching itself apart, both internally and outwardly. And my soul seemed to be splitting along with my head. My consciousness tore inside my mind, unable to fully choose which side to escape to.

A disintegrating line cut right down the middle of my skull. I fell to my knees and held my head as it tore apart!

I expected blood and brains to spill down my face, but instead blue and red protoplasm slinked out of my head and slowly pulled apart from each other. The red and blue became two separate entities. The red was from the left side of my head, and the blue was from my right.

They were both still connected to my consciousness, because I could feel it as an anchor. I could feel myself being pulled to the left and to the right and then back again. The protoplasm began to show expressions as faces formed out of the gooey matter. And they began fighting like two king cobras, slashing at each other with teeth that grew longer and sharper as each second passed.

They fought as I was going insane.

I screamed in indescribable torment. The pain became too unbearable, and my vision failed as darkness overwhelmed me. I fell hard enough for my head to feel the cement under my apartment's thin carpet.

I faded away, not knowing which side won.

I came to and just looked around for a while. But all I could see was my entertainment center from my vantage on the floor. I crawled towards the love seat and pulled myself up.

I looked around at the normal reality of it all and realized I had turned down the one chance at finding the truth. I was shattered. Devastated. Lost.

Even after all I went through, I couldn't sleep and I quickly became a mess. Crying, laughing, screaming—nothing I did made me feel right.

And then I noticed something horrifying. I noticed my mind was putting me down and having me think the worst about everything. I tried thinking I didn't believe all my own negativity. But even as I thought that, a part of myself continued to batter me down.

I heard me say that I hated myself, that I'm a liar who lies to myself all the time. The thoughts kept coming and I had no choice but to listen. I freaked out. I've always been by myself in my head and have never heard other voices, especially not ones that just wanted to ruin me.

I walked into my bedroom and flopped down on the bed, still listening to my mind beat me down. I wanted to fall asleep but couldn't. So I just laid there and listened.

"Why am I thinking this? I don't feel this way about myself."

Then I heard it. I actually fucking heard it. It said, "Yes, you do."

"I'm a good man, or at least I try to be," I retorted.

"No you're not. You're an evil man up to evil things."

My heart beat faster as I suspected my trips to the other side had brought back a demon. I thought I'd been possessed. My mind was a flutter of everything and anything. It was like having two hundred butterflies flying around in my skull, every butterfly was a thought or an idea that was either against each other or flew in harmony.

I jumped out of bed and stormed into the living room, pacing.

It became quiet suddenly. I stood there for seven seconds when I heard, "I'm worthless."

"I'm not worthless," I said aloud.

"Yes you are. You're nothing in this world."

The explanation I still come up with is possession. Full-blown, spin-your-head, puke pea soup, in-the-Devil's custody. I calmed down and tried talking to it.

"Who are you?"

Silence.

"What do you think you're doing?"

Nothing. I decided to stay silent.

"I think I should jerk off."

I didn't think that! Sexual thoughts were the furthest thing from my mind at that moment. (Thinking you're possessed sort of tames the libido!).

Then I heard, "I'm such an asshole. I hate myself and everything about me."

I felt it! Dear God, I felt it! I felt where those last thoughts originated! They came from my left side! I've never felt that before. I continued to pay attention.

This time, I heard, "It's okay. It's all right. You're a good man."

I began to become more peaceful. My worries eased until I heard from my left side again.

"I hate myself."

My right side countered, "It's okay. Just don't listen to him."

I tilted my head down, in a total freefall of reality. Shit! I was not only possessed; I was possessed by two beings! One apparently good, and one apparently bad! I held my head in my hands as I began to ask questions.

"What are you doing?"

"Fucking you up."

"Trying to help you."

"What are you?" I asked.

A second passes and I hear, "God." "The Devil."

I knew what sides each came from. "Great!" I told myself. "I've been trying to find God, and I found the Devil as well!"

Now pacing, I asked, "What do I do now?"

"Relax."

"Kill yourself!"

I begin to cry, lost in a new world where I can suddenly hear God and the Devil.

"I can't take this!" I scream. I only hear one response this time.

"Then you must kill yourself. It is the only thing that will bring you relief. You wanted this and now you got it."

I got up and walked over to my computer.

* * *

You sit in the usual place in my apartment, behind the desk. You watch the younger me approach, and you jump out of the leather chair, trying to slink your way towards the kitchen in time. You pray I don't bump into you, but I do. My shoulder goes right through you without even a ripple. You jump into the kitchen to find the older me leaning against the stove.

"Don't worry, my younger self can't hear or feel you right now. I am, er, he is too busy fighting the personal demons."

"If you watch me on the computer," I continue, "I'm going to be pulling up sites on possession and on talking to God and the Devil."

Sitting behind the desk, the young me screams, "Shut the fuck up!" The words are aimed at two beings not in the room.

I explain things in the kitchen.

"Most people would have killed themselves by now. I'm really going nuts behind that desk, arguing with both of them. I don't know if the voices were actually myself, or if I am possessed by the Holy Spirit and the Unholy Spirit at the same time. I could have easily split my personality with what I was doing. So I was trying to cope, to learn and to figure it out. Maybe it was a puzzle? Maybe I was just insane or became a schizophrenic. I was experiencing what some schizophrenics have been said to experience so maybe I went mad during all of this. Let's just say, this moment in my life, I was utterly and hopelessly insane."

Sitting behind the desk, I continue screaming, "How am I supposed to do anything if you're constantly talking to me! Stop fucking with me!"

As we stand in the kitchen, I open the refrigerator, looking for something to eat. It's pretty barren as the empty cold box stares back at me.

"Oops, I forgot. I never kept much in the refrigerator."

I close the door and lean against the nearest wall. It's easy to find, as the small kitchen is two feet wide by eight foot long.

"Today was the day my mind split," I tell you. "Freud brought up the whole Id and Superego analysis. I didn't really know anything about it at the time; all I knew was that I was thirty years old and felt insane. I came across a lot of religious websites that day. They explained possession by the Devil but not by God."

"I also tried looking for scientific answers. I began to look up psychology. Although it was growing exponentially, the Internet was still in its infancy at that time. But I did manage to look up Freud and his ideas on the Id and the Superego."

* * *

During the next week, I argued and fought with my screaming Devil side, as it tried talking me into killing or into killing myself. It made me feel horrible.

Meanwhile, my good side stayed mostly quiet and never lifted its voice beyond a whisper for support.

Both sides rooted for me to choose a side and to either better my life or destroy it. I searched the web but never found anyone who experienced such a dramatic splitting of the mind. I was probably looking for the type of account that you're reading in this book now.

I had either created a dialogue with God and the Devil with no way to shut down the communication, or my personality split into the Id and the Superego, my higher moral self and my base instinct.

But here's a puzzler about the Freud approach. If my so-called Devil side was the Id, why was it harping on killing myself or killing others? Why was it calling me names? Why was it trying to destroy me from the inside out? There was no pleasure in any of this. If this was the Id, it should be wanting me to seek pure selfish pleasure.

This wasn't my pleasure principal coming to life. This was something more devious, more chaotic than I could understand. My mind continued to fight and my spirit was desperately trying to stay alive. I searched for everything I could find on the subject; otherwise, I was going to end up in a rubber room with a nice new straight jacket for my fall fashions, but for my winter fashions as well.

Before this, my consciousness had been alone with my memories and knowledge. I had chugged though life, alone in my mind, doing whatever I wanted, whenever I wanted.

My unconscious mind burst out of me, and all my fears, selfish desires and immoral wishes became a distinct and separate reality. At the same time, my morals became higher and even all encompassing, taking over my personality. I could see myself being the best I could be, while a part of me wanted to be at my lowest. The true shame was my Demons were a hell of a lot stronger than my Angels.

Let me tell you a little of what I learned and made my own. Here it goes:

The Id and the Superego are more scientific ways of considering the Devil and God, or personal angels and demons. Science has turned the relationship between God, the Devil, and you into a viewpoint for all to understand without the framework of religious belief to sidetrack the layperson into another whole realm of thinking.

The Id is directed into the most primitive, basic desires; lust, greed, envy, pride, sloth, wrath, gluttony and even death. The Superego guides you towards chastity, temperance, charity, diligence, patience, kindness, humility and even life.

Freud was just trying to map the human mind but instead came across something inside many of us that hadn't been documented before. I say "many of us" because some people don't seem to have a conscience and have committed the world's greatest horrors and atrocities. To commit murder, torture, rape, or genocide is pure Id and the Devil. Every aspect of every situation that is wrong comes from either of those two places.

Science and psychology were not looking to verify religious notions. But they did. They weren't trying to verify the war between God and the Devil but again, they did. Freud was just trying to make us all better. He was trying to figure out the happening in our mind. He was charting previously unknown territory, and he found a bigger continent within us all that he never could have fathomed. If you think about it, it has made us better and will continue to do so.

Yes, he was wrong about a lot of things. He was doing coke and talking to himself a mile a minute. But look what he accomplished.

THE QUEST BEGINS WITH A STEP THROUGH THE LEVEL OF ATROCITY

Now before we get ahead of ourselves, as I want to, I need to say I am relating exactly what happened when it happened. I'm not including here the insights I learned ten years later. I am telling you what I was thinking as it was unfolding. I've learned a lot more since then, and it will come later. A baby has to crawl before it can walk, and at this time, I was a baby. This was just the beginning of reasoning and understanding.

I understand how crazy this sounds at times, and my journey might even be called sacrilegious by certain sects. But my heart was on one simple track, and that was to find God.

Again, my personal demons were stronger then my personal angels. At the time, they were God and the Devil—they even called themselves that. And it was even more confusing: while the thoughts from God always seemed like they were from Him, the thoughts from the Devil pretended as if they were my own. I was exhausted by the internal combat I faced in every waking moment.

I was trying to hang out with friends or family, but the battle inside my head was killing me inside. Every minute was excruciating, as I didn't even know if my thoughts were my own. And I had to keep it to myself. If I stood up in a restaurant and began to fight with myself, I'd be locked away as a mental case. I've seen the homeless walk around, arguing with themselves. I now understand where they are coming from.

In fact, they could even be exactly where I was: stuck there and not being able move ahead in life because they didn't understand what was going on in their heads. We don't teach metaphysics in school so Average Joe has no clue if he comes across this sort of actuality.

So I bided my time until I was alone. Then I would argue with myself. I'd talk to God and yell at the Devil. If I hadn't been working from home, recording video tapes for people as my business, I wouldn't have been able to go insane and still make a living if that's what we call it. Imagine if that's the problem of most of the psychiatric patients in the world. Imagine if people are actually taking to entities and God and other beings beyond.

Let's imagine these entities are masquerading as the people that they are terrorizing in their own head?

Now… let's imagine that they would tell you, you're somebody else.

Now, let's imagine that they would tell you about germs, bugs, communism, terrorism, depression, danger, murder, rape, death, kill, kill… kill!

How can anyone live his or her life in a loop?

What I mean by a loop is: a strong, subconscious idea that circles around every real idea or thought, no matter if it's good or bad. Slowly squeezing the life out of it and replacing it as the original idea. Yes, this is an understanding of our mind that I have understood. I see it every day and in everyone I see. It gets worse as we get older, a lot worse

I pray none of you have to go through this. I've read that this usually happens in the teenage years and earlier. The younger the mind, the easier the split is between the Id and the Superego. The older the mind, the more set it is in its ways; it doesn't want to change.

Perhaps not coincidentally, in *The Matrix,* Morpheus tells Neo, "There is a rule that we do not free a mind once it reaches a certain age. It is dangerous. They have trouble letting go. Their mind turns against them. I've seen it happen."

As for me, my internal volume was turned up really high—as loud as my own voice—drowning out everything around me, and sometimes that was the problem. It'd been a week of pure schizophrenic chaos for me. I couldn't concentrate or focus because the voices were just so fucking loud.

Then one night came and I made a decision to open all of the doors in one night. I knew I would go further than I ever had before. I was ready to die to truly find God and I wasn't going to stop. I already made myself insane so what more could happen?

I had a hundred count sheet of acid that only had twenty hits left. I went and bought five boxes of Whip Its and a bunch of punch balloons. I visited the laser disc store and bought a copy of *The End of Days* because I knew the Rob Zombie video *Superbeast* was on it that I'd watched the first time I met that entity. I suspected the hallucinogenic visuals would open up a hypnotic state within myself if I repeated it long enough.

My God side was telling me I was the one, that I would become famous and help millions of people. My Devil side… you already knew what he was saying, so I ate eight hits of acid and set up a lot of balloons and began my search for God. I popped in the laserdisc and made myself comfortable. I have always heard that if you ask, doors will be opened for you. I slowly opened the biggest door of my life.

* * *

We find ourselves thrust into a vortex of light and sound. We both fall upwards towards the darkness, which envelops our minds as shards of reality splinter all around us. We begin to see humans, but at first, they are more primitive than ourselves. We then witness a frightening montage of orgiastic violence:

* An early man held a tree branch. He lifted it high and brought it down onto another's head, cracking open the skull while brains splattered everywhere.

* Two Israelites grabbed another in a dark alley. The third man had his body slit from throat to spine with a blunt knife. Blood squirted everywhere as he slumped to the ground. The other two rifled through his pockets as he died.

* In a Roman coliseum, several people were tied to stakes. Lions were circling them as one lunged and sank its teeth into a victim's neck. The lion shreds his flesh off his body.

* Ancient armies were clashing together. Swords were waving in the air when they weren't hacking off limbs or being thrust into bodies.

* A man in a loincloth was tied to the ground while being ripped apart by vultures. One of the birds buried its beak into his eye socket and pulled out the eyeball, trying to swallow it whole.

* A man was being ritually castrated in a ceremony for the good of royalty. Another was sacrificing his son in an ancient ceremony to Baal. Another man was being impaled with a huge stake and lifted up in front of a town. His screams bellowed out as each movement slid the stake deeper inside of him.

* A woman whose face was filled with pustules was ripping out her eyes in a desperate attempt to no longer see.

* Two men were dueling with swords when one swiped at the other's stomach. His intestines slipped out of his body as he attempted desperately to hold them in.

* Waves of European soldiers attacked each other as cannonballs ripped into the legions of men. Body upon body lay in all manner of decomposition, disease and mortification.

* Slaves were split from neck to crotch while still alive. Their guts were pulled out in an array of gore and blood.

* A woman was being tied to the ground as ants ate her alive for committing adultery. Another was in seizures from a snakebite as the poison ran through her veins.

* A man was strapped in a guillotine and the executioner pulled the lever. The blade came down, chopping off his head. The crowd screamed with delight as the executioner lifted the dismembered head to the audience, hoping the facial features were still moving.

* A man and a woman were tied to a stake and burned alive while the surrounding people screamed "Witch!"

* Several people were in a dungeon as priests were torturing them, trying to make them confess. A tongue was ripped out, a back was broken. A woman was slammed on the rack. The screams of the innocent wailed as the chuckles of the damned echoed in the damp room.

* Infantrymen shot and stabbed anyone in a different uniform. Bombs dropped on innocent families. Mortars ripped into buildings, devastating and destroying men, women and children in a disgusting display of force. A tank ran over a soldier, cutting him in half. Ships sunk, dragging men to the bottom and drowning them as they pushed and clawed the people in the way of the doors.

* Massive graves of Chinese were set ablaze as the dead were lined up for over a mile from the invading army's front line. More people lined up in showers as poisonous gas flooded out of shower nozzles. Others were being used as experiments. Pressurized chambers, rape, torture, amputation and slow agonizing death were the fate of some. Hunger and disease took the rest. People were lined up, front to back, as guns were fired to see how far bullets would go. Teeth were pulled while charting the excruciating pain factor. People were being boiled alive, frozen and stripped of their skin.

* Japanese citizens were staring at the sky as the high-pitched wail of an atomic bomb whistled its way to the ground. The explosion melted the eyes of everyone in a mile radius as their skin bubbled and burst into flames. Some were disintegrated immediately while others, farther away, were thrust into brick walls with shrapnel.

* Men butchered mothers and their children for being in the wrong village at the wrong time. Others were trying to commit genocide as wave after wave of teenagers, wearing a couple of pieces of militia insignia, were trying to cleanse the world of another race. Hands were cut off for stealing. Eyes were gouged out for looking at royalty. Heads were hacked off with swords. Scalps were taken with glee while whole villages were hacked and shot to death for land or food.

* Men stepped on land mines and were forced to play Russian roulette until it became deadly. Women with razor blades in their vaginas seduced soldiers, to slice their cocks apart during sex. Mothers held down daughters, cutting their clits off. Others mutilated themselves for the approval of their elders in the same village. Parents were eating the rotting flesh of their kids to keep their memory alive, while others killed the children of other tribes to eat them for their power.

* Men and children, strapped with bombs, walked into crowded places, setting themselves off in an array of shrapnel and gore that killed everyone in a 25-foot radius.

* Husbands were killing their wives as wives mutilated their husbands in their sleep. Children where hacking their parents to death. Other children were killing their peers as if it were a game. Lonely people were shooting others because they hated themselves, while others were killing people for political

motives. The insane were killing others, as the depressed were killing themselves, hanging, slicing, poisoning and shooting just to put a stop to their lives of unredeemable agony.

As the scenes of death and carnage float away from us, I notice I am drooling on myself. I wipe my mouth with my hand and spread it on my jeans. We sit there for a second, stunned.

I turn to you, and your head is in your hands. I hear you faintly sobbing, or is it laughter? I can't tell, and I think I'm better off not knowing.

"I'm sorry for thrusting you into that," I say. "I know it's something you didn't want to see and if you did, I understand. I'm going to keep you as a normal reader from now on until the time is right."

You look up and want to say something, but you don't. I wave my hand slowly in front of your face and your eyes close. You hear me make myself comfortable in my chair as I begin again.

* * *

I found myself standing up and shaking my fist at the truth of reality that we don't all see. Violence from the ages flashed before me in an array of atrocity. I was excited, exasperated and totally clueless to what was really going on. Why did I just witness this? Was it to make me more impressionable or more open to what was coming next? Did it open certain synapses in my mind, awakening a section of my brain that I will need later? Was it a warning sign for me to stop? Violence usually makes a person run away. But I knew I couldn't.

So I set everything up again and I opened another door.

HE COMES AND SHOWS DESPAIR, EXHILARATION, ULTIMATE POWERS AND ISOLATION

I woke up, totally blind. A crushing weight enveloped my body. As my senses came to, I found I was buried or what seemed like it. I couldn't open my eyes because of the crushing weight. I could only wiggle my body a bit. It felt as if I was trapped under mud or a thick slime. As I moved around, my body created more wiggle room.

I don't remember breathing, just the struggle to get out. The substance that jailed me began to lift away as my body became more forceful. I could feel the weight ease as my hand broke the surface. I made my way towards the light on the other side.

I broke free! My head lifted out of the muck and into the daylight. My lungs filled with the sweet air of eternity as I pulled myself out of my encasement and onto my carpet. I watched as the slimy prison pulled into itself, slowly dissipating. I stood up, finding a familiar entity dancing around. I stared at him, taking him all in, and indeed it was the angel in the Technicolor dreamcoat disguised as Rob Zombie.

The music pumped as it raised its hands, urging me to look around. I then realized I could see through my apartment walls. I could see my neighbors on every side of me. I could see further too, as all the trees, fences, walls and furniture were then totally invisible to me. Nothing was visible except people, for miles around.

Let me try to explain it to you like this: It was as if I was suddenly transported to the middle of a giant desert that was totally flat. Everything was gone except for the people, doing what they were doing. Living life, watching TV, making love or sleeping in their beds—but there wasn't anything I could see that was material. Walls, everything that was a solid I could see through. Every soul, on the other hand, I could see perfectly.

All the people I saw were wrapped in the slime I had just broken out of, and no one seemed to know any better. I was looking at my neighbors when the

Entity moved into my sight. His long psychedelic coat pulsed to the beat, and my mind drank it all in.

"You can see all the people around you who are asleep," he said. "None of them has been able to break through their own conscious shells. If they're lucky, they'll break through the second seal. Everyone has four barriers to break through to get where you are now. They may be ignorant to all universal truths and perceive themselves as completely separate and totally independent individuals in this cosmos."

My mind tried to grasp what he was saying.

"At the second level, they do have some logical perception of cosmic truths, but they don't have enough prescience or inspiration to do anything about it."

All around me, I saw friends, neighbors and strangers encased in something horrible, as if the slimy shell fed off the host. I turned to look back into the Entity's eyes and actually caught them, staring into him this time. I was amazed when we locked eyes and he stared back into me, allowing me to see into him and even past him. I forgot at this time, that when you look into something, it looks back into you. His eyes swirled and pulsated with eyes of untold authority. I could only stare and listen to its words as his eyes swirled into my own self.

He said, "You are now at the top of the human curve. You are now able to control people by influence."

I sat back on my couch. I looked right and saw my neighbor, Jimmy. He seemed to be watching TV. It's hard to say; he was floating about fifteen feet away from me, staring at a spot in space for a long time. I figured it was his TV since I'd been to his house before and knew the layout.

The entity looked at me, with blazing eyes and said, "Give it a try."

I looked at Jimmy and wanted him to stand and change the channel on the TV.

Jimmy stood and walked to where his TV should have been and reached out his hand. He began pushing something unseen. I laughed and looked over to my other neighbor and thought he should go for a ride.

Jose stood up out of what was probably his bed (he was laying down, floating in the air) and moved his arms around as if getting dressed. He walked towards his front door, meandering his way through invisible hallways and rooms. He walked out through the parking lot, opened something, and sat down in midair.

He started up the invisible car, which I could hear, as it turned out. He backed up then drove away, although it really looked more like flying.

"It's not going to be that easy in what you would call real life," the entity said. "You will have to use superiority, confidence and guile to persuade them as you just did."

"You were doing it already," it continued, "But you were never actually taught."

"I can understand now."

He turned to me and waved his coat. He flung it over me, saying, "Then let's open the next door. Your lessons are truly beginning."

The dreamcoat lay over my face as I was whisked away to someplace new.

I found myself driving a convertible in the middle of a psychedelic city. Buildings grew, streets shrank and the entity (God?) was on the hood of the car, screaming at me the whole time.

Every imaginable color erupted all around me, as people's souls zoomed past me, leaving wakes I could feel.

He yelled, "Do it! Show me your power!"

I lifted my hand and power began to form out of nothingness. It turned into a ball of liquid energy, and I let it build strength until I felt it hit critical mass. The car barreled down the road as I got ready to throw it. God was grabbing onto the windshield while kneeling on the hood.

"Do it!"

I held the steering wheel with my left hand, and my right hand threw the energy ball. It grew and flashed in flight. I grabbed the steering wheel with both hands and watched my energy ball devastate everything in its path. I was enraptured at the destruction.

The ball quickly left my sight, and although I could no longer see it, there was devastation as far as my mind could see. It apparently wasn't done, and God said, "Wait for it."

I slowed the convertible to a crawl and looked at the destruction. I heard the screams of the innocent as fire and flames continued to char everything that had been in its way. I began to hear chaos rumbling behind me.

The ball of psychic energy I created was actually coming around again. "Did it just go all around the world?"

Apparently, it did. As it came closer, buildings shattered into dust, roads were ripped apart and people disintegrated. The ball of energy plowed ahead of me, continuing to annihilate everything. I could feel it begin to break apart and slowly lose its power. I saw it hit a skyscraper and dissipate. The building was hit hard enough to crack and begin to fall. It took out all the other buildings as it slammed against the city blocks. Dust and debris scattered everywhere.

God was just smiling. Then he was gone. I sat alone in the car, amazed, when I began to hear it.

Sirens wailed and people ran all over the city, trying to rescue those left alive. I turned around and saw the same devastation behind me. Then I felt it:

The souls cried out in pain and with fear. The souls' outpouring shocked my nervous system as the realization of what I had done finally hit home.

My psychic energy not only devastated this city but went around the earth, carving out a swath of devastation until it returned. Who knows how many cities or people it hurt? I didn't know or realize what was happening but my soul felt it in an unimaginable wave of guilt and horror.

Tears ran down my face, and the guilt of killing on this magnitude was more than my mind could handle.

I was thrust back into my living room with a dread of reality that shook my whole apartment.

I really don't know why I was shown that, or even why I did it. Why would it make me feel the death of over a hundred thousand beings, all across the world? Why would a person need to know that kind of anguish? Why?

If it was just a lesson about how the things we do can destroy others, it didn't make any sense. Was it just to show me I had a power but had to use it responsibly? I really didn't know and didn't care at this point. I knew I had to continue.

So I opened another door and walked through to the other side.

I found myself alone in a void of nothingness, floating in the darkness of space. I was left alone to ponder my existence. Fear crept up on me until I saw a speck of white light in the distance. It slowly came into better view. I paid attention to what I felt emanating from it.

I felt a previously unknown joy and happiness coming from the white light. I began to sense it was a city, a glorious metropolis that shimmered as pure light in the darkness. I felt the beautiful souls of that city. I felt the wonder and gratitude of those who resided there.

It was enough to make me cry, but I didn't. This is where my soul began to turn. I began to feel bitterness towards those in the city before me. Resentment turned to anger and anger turned to wrath. It bubbled within me like a seething cauldron of hate that began to spill into this reality.

I knew they were blessed even before they were born and I hated them for it. I have never felt the hate of the damned until that moment. I seethed and felt that the damned should have justice. We *needed* justice if we were damned before we were even born.

I became aware that my skin was peeling away from the muscles of my legs. Bright golden metal began to rip out from under my skin, covering my legs, morphing my hatred into a physical reality. I screamed as muscle turned to metal, metal to weaponry. My arms split up the middle, and my bones multiplied. Skin tissue spasmed and became various electrical components. My blood seized up, turning into black oil to lubricate my new form.

My forearms tore apart, and in their place, cannons assembled out of skin and bone. The pain was off the charts, but I screamed with delight as my body became the ultimate weapon for retribution.

I laughed as my wrath was made whole. That is, until it crept up to my face.

When the armor hit my neck, the flesh slowed its transformation. I knew I couldn't stop it, so I said, "Yes!"

Golden cables tore out from the back of my head, piercing my skull from the inside. They pulled to each side of my head and crawled to my temples.

91

More cables slashed out of my skin, darting about, looking to strike into the windows of my soul.

I knew then I needed to kill all of those whom I could never be. I said, "Do it!"

The cables plunged into the sides of my eyes and buried themselves deep into my sockets. I felt them turn behind my retinas, and offshoots of cables dug everywhere into my vision. My head split open and the golden alloy emerged from my skull, covering what was left of me. My suit of armor was complete.

Still floating in space, my body was now a weapon whose power has only been seen by the likes of God and the Devil. I felt cannons and guns whirring around, connected to me. A small plasma cannon was at my wrist, and as I considered it, it became bigger. All the weapons began to twist and grow into stronger, more sophisticated weaponry brought into existence by my mind.

There was no fear, just a need for death and destruction. I flew towards the pure white light with amazing speed. The closer I got, the more magnificent it became. The white purity of the city would dazzle your eyes with columns stretching to eternity. Walls raced to everywhere and doorways opened to everything. The souls there were happy and they marveled at their own existence.

That is, until I flew in, discharging weapons of destruction everywhere around me. The people began to scatter as blasts from my shoulders curved in deadly nets of electrified death. Those caught in it were cut to pieces. Other lasers widened their streams, taking out more people in an inescapable wave of mortality they didn't know of or even understand.

Sharp metallic tentacles erupted from my back, taking out the souls I didn't shoot. Blood and gore ran through the streets as a torrential flood of death overcame everyone.

Missiles fired out of my back towards buildings around me. The devastation was becoming more apparent.

There wasn't any resistance. It was just a slaughter. I fired wave after wave of mortars and rockets at everything around me. I wanted to raze this place to the ground and I wanted those pure white streets to run red with the blood of the innocent.

After it was, I stopped, hovering in the middle of the square. My anger hadn't subsided and I still wanted death. I looked below me and saw the limbs and bodies of those I had killed. I relished it. The bloodlust within me was indescribable as I continued to kill, slaughter and maim anything I could see. I felt that they deserved it. I felt anger, wrath for being brought into this world without a chance. Being created and left with fucked-up people as my guides. Being left with a society, not giving me any hope. And I had done the right thing and lost every time.

Then I had found these souls, these far too wonderful souls. Souls who were jubilant and carefree, actually thankful for every breath they took, happy to find themselves alive. Not struggling to survive or hoping for the quickness of death, with whatever they worked for ready to disappear.

I floated there for another moment and looked at my destruction.

"Why would I do this after feeling the heart-wrenching sadness of what I experienced before?"

With this thought, I opened the last door.

I found myself in an ancient cathedral. Its wood, marble and stone was glistening from the light coming through the stained-glass windows. I was standing in the middle of the pews, looking at the cross and the altar at the end of it. I marveled at the wonder and sanctity of the church when He came in.

It was God, but this time He was pissed. His colorful coat whisked behind Him as He strode to the middle of the church. He stopped 20 feet away from me and looked me straight in the eyes.

"This is what people are worshipping!" he said. "This is what people think God is. This ends up sending more people to Hell than you can believe."

I stared at Him. I didn't know what to do since I had been searching for God, and now I knew I'd found Him. I found this entity while searching for God, and He was teaching me, showing me that my reality isn't true, that I am capable of severe destruction, that I can know unforgettable remorse.

I experienced so much on my search for God that I trusted in Him. So I stood and listened.

He said, "Witness what people believe in their hearts and what they worship. It's not God, it's something else!"

With that, He waved His hand and showed me what was behind the altar. A face emerged and slowly became real. It was the face of an old man. It was our common image of God—a bearded, angry old man. Its eyes were downcast. A frown was on his face. In this face, the power of God was wrath and not love. It was the face of people threatening others for committing sin. It was the God who destroyed Sodom and Gomorrah. It was the God who cursed Moses for saying a miracle was his doing. I could see this God abandoning those before me and kicking my kind out of Eden and into the cruel, hard world. To work, suffer, and die. I saw the angry God who just wanted to punish, torture and damn the people whom He had created.

I saw the God that some parents threaten their kids with. I saw the God that will torture, for all eternity anyone born of a different faith. I saw anger, hate and pain, in the God I saw on that pedestal in that wondrous church.

God said, "I need your help, destroying this false idol of God!"

With that, He fired multi-colored blasts from his hands, towards the face of God. His lightning hit its mark, and it pushed to its limit, but it couldn't destroy the face. I knew what it was doing because I did it earlier.

I raised my hand and felt my energized soul begin to charge. It was as if every part of my life was coalescing in my hand. I felt the power build up towards its critical mass. As soon as it hit, I threw it towards the false figurehead of God.

I didn't let go like before. It was a steady stream of destruction. I was not going to let up since my God counted on me. Together, we worked on destroying the false figurehead, towards the goal of destroying the fictitious God of everyone's mind.

The face bruised and withered and finally imploded with a scream. Anger and hate emanated in its final moments. Its bellow withdrew as it folded inside of itself. It flowed backwards into an abyss of darkness, disappearing.

The church glowed and hummed. I slumped towards the floor but caught myself on a pew. I steadied myself and lifted my eyes toward my God, but He was gone.

I looked around the church and noticed everything in it: The collection plate on the seat next to me. A piece of gum under a pew. The smell of dust on one of the Bibles in a cubbyhole. I took a deep breath and stood there. And then I was gone.

ANOTHER DREAM COME TRUE, PARANOIA AND POSSESSION BY GOD

I woke at 8 a.m. the next day. I never wake up in the morning. I usually sleep until afternoon. I've always enjoyed the night. The night was the time when magic happened. The night was when the darkness kept you from being seen.

I stretched and looked at the sun through the blinds. A thought struck me. I suddenly felt the urge to open a video store. Not just any video store but a cult video store. When I say "cult," I mean kung fu, gore, anime, and everything in between. Not a single mainstream film in the house. Just the crazy shit I've been selling that I can find from all over the world.

I had dreamed of having a cool video store since I was twelve. I got out of bed and shuffled towards the shower. I turned on the water and let it get warm, and I was actually at peace for the first time in a long time. My personal angel and demon were giving me a temporary reprieve.

So my mind was free to race at two hundred miles an hour. Had I really met God? Was he really showing me all this? Why am I thinking about trying to open a video store without any money? Why do I have this urge?

The water was hot so I climbed in. While scrubbing myself clean, I knew I had the power to get off my ass and do something I'd always wanted to do. Even though I was making great money, I knew it couldn't last for long. DVD had just premiered a year ago, and lots of the films I was copying were coming out. So I knew I couldn't bootleg VCR tapes forever.

I wanted a stable life, and opening up a store would take a great investment on my part, but I felt as if I could take on the world. I toweled myself off, brushed my teeth and found some clothes. I put them on and walked out another door.

Now, I lived in Tampa, FL, US of A. There were a lot of potential places to set up a video store, but Blockbuster and Hollywood Video chain locations were everywhere. I didn't want to be in any competition, just to find a place where cool, hip, "now"-type people would enjoy a store of this kind.

The obvious choice seemed an area called Ybor City. It's Florida's version of Bourbon Street, just not as big or jazzy. It had clubs, bars, cigars, and upscale (and downscale) restaurants for the hipsters and tourists. A party place where they closed the streets every night because so many people got drunk, fought, and partied their asses off.

I drove to Ybor, wondering how I might be able to afford it. The place was always full and real estate was at a total premium since GameWorks and Victoria Secret moved in. Waiting lists must be by the hundreds at the time. I knew I would be terribly lucky to find a store.

You'd think my mind would be on other things, like the events of a few hours ago. But I was instead looking for retail space. I didn't know what to think about the night's events, but it felt like God was throwing me a bone. That's how it felt. Since the voices inside my head subsided—or maybe they were just pretending to be me!—I don't know but I went with it. I always just go with it.

I pulled onto the Ybor City exit and found the main street, Seventh. I began looking into each space to see if anything was for rent. Nothing was. But I was going to find something. I felt it. Just as I felt in my heart I had done something spectacular the night before. Not many people find God, commune with Him, or live His lessons without stopping or walking away from a challenge.

I came to the actual end of Ybor City. Nothing was for rent or sale. I stopped at the red light and was just about to feel dejected when I saw it: An empty storefront, right on the corner of Seventh and Twenty Second Street. It was right at the end of the party zone. There was a huge parking lot in front of it for a Cuban restaurant. I pulled in and was still in a daze as I approached the door. A sign indicated the number to call, and I took out my cell phone and gave it a ring.

The landlord answered and told me he would be there in 30. It was more like two. Before I knew it, I was signing a contract in less than an hour. No deposit, no upfront. Just $725 a month. A thousand square feet of retail space was mine. I had the keys that day.

I called my friends to see who would help. One very special friend—let's call him "The Man"—helped me immeasurably. He had a side business (it's where I got my acid, if you catch my drift) so he could keep his own hours. He helped, not for money and not for promises, but because he thought that the store should be built. The Man loved gore films and he wanted to share the love of gore, death, murder and fucked-up shit. He loved to find lost, banned gore films like I did. It was always a kick to show something that has been much-rumored but rarely seen. The Man was my right-hand man. Even his girlfriend came, helping more than she should have.

It was a ton of work. We bought particleboard for the plastic shelf units I found for ten cents apiece. I bought lasers, strobe lights, and a fog machine to make the store an "experience." I decided to make the place R-rated and not admit kids under 17 without a parent. That was a bit of a gimmick, but then again, the crap I was renting and selling was brutal, and the DVD and VCR boxes showed it. So I didn't want to fuck up a good thing with Johnny Law, much less fuck up an innocent soul.

So I had stencils made to put a big "Rated R" on the front door. It was menacing and exactly how I wanted it: A retail store with teeth.

A funny thing happened on the way to building that store. When I was being issued a phone number, I asked my phone provider if the number 666 was available. The phone guy laughed and said, "Any and all numbers with 666 are available. No one wants them. You actually want one?"

"Yeah. I'm opening a cult video store specializing in horror films. I think it would be a kick and easy for my customers to remember."

My number became 246-4666. I couldn't get 666-4666 because there isn't exchange with "666" anywhere in the United States. So I got the next best thing. I put a huge sign with the numbers in the front windows. It read:

Video Mayhem! Cult, Gore, Anime and Kung Fu flicks for the Criminally Insane!
Phone Number 246-4666.

I was still making money from bootlegs on the web, and it almost gave me enough for the store, but I needed more cash. My Mom came into the picture and lent me some of her inheritance from my Uncle John. It was actually from my grandfather but he took my mother out of the will for some stupid reason. My uncle was gracious and Christian enough to give her half. My Mom turned around and gave me a third of it, about $10,000 to help. And it did. I could buy plenty of new DVDs for the store. I slowly paid back my Mom as the years went by. Since Mom was pretty poor, the loan was a big deal for her and me.

The Man and I built the store from a dream to a reality. When it was finished, we decided to celebrate. I thanked God for the help and for the initiative.

The Man broke out a bag of hydro, and I wanted to celebrate. I'd smoked only a tiny bit of pot while working on the store, so I was ready to relax and get fucked up. The Man broke out a full bowl of crippy. We smoked it and then did a couple of more.

As I took the last hit of pot, holding it in my lungs to get everything from it, it hit me like a ton of fucking bricks: Shame, guilt, sin, lust, Hell. My Id, my personal Devil was screaming in my ear. I couldn't enjoy the buzz, because my own mind was trying to destroy me.

"What's wrong dude?" The Man asked.

"It feels like I am going out of my fucking mind!"

"Don't worry. It's crippy, dude. You'll calm down."

"No, this is different. I've never had a problem with pot before"

"Yeah, I know. I've never see you freak out no matter what kind of drug it is."

Now, The Man knew I'd met God. I'd told everyone by that time. I had a lot of friends dismiss me as a fool. Some listened, then found it too heavy to continue. Others? Well, I've saved a soul here and there.

"I hear voices, dude, and they're fucking me up!" I told The Man.

"I'm going to take off. If you're actually having a fit inside, it might be better for me to not be here. I'll see you tomorrow in the morning. If you're not here, I will open the store and try to finish this place up." The Man grabbed his jacket off the counter and headed for the door.

I said, "Man, thanks."

"No worries, just get your head together before tomorrow."

With that, he left. The Man didn't laugh at me or do any of the usual stoner-type of funniness everyone does to each other. He took it at face value and left without making a big deal out of it. The front door closed and I sprang into action.

I jumped up and locked the door. I wrestled with my personal demons for the rest of the night in my brand new store. As the buzz wore off, so did my internal struggle. I thank God it did.

I was so grateful for all that had happened to me in my God quest that I bought a Bible that night. I'd only heard stories that The Bible was His book, dictated to others throughout the ages. I didn't want to die and meet God and have him ask me, "So Stephen, you found me and changed your life. How did you like the only book I ever wrote? Was there anything more I could have done with it? Give me your honest review."

There was no way in Hell that I wanted to tell my Creator that I didn't read His book. So I bought one at the local Wal-Mart. It was a King James Edition with a leatherbound cover and gilded gold pages. I don't know what the clerk thought about a man buying a Bible at 3 a.m., and I didn't care. I just needed the Book in my possession. I had experienced God on a personal level, and I had heard His voice, and I'd done what I was supposed to. Now, I needed His words. I took it home and plopped it down on my desk, to read later.

I'm still surprised I didn't pick it up and read it then. A personal encounter with God changes me to an unrecognizable new person, and I don't read it? I personally think I was supposed to have that Bible for when the exact time came. The time came, but it took its slow, sweet time.

I haven't mentioned my change in behavior yet. After my first experience, and especially after later ones, I had many people comment and say I was like a new human being. And I was; I listened to everyone with a new heart, and I never judged anyone but tried to give them guidance as I now saw it. If they didn't understand, I didn't judge them for that. It felt wonderful to talk to everyone on every level, no matter where they were in life. I guess that's when I noticed I could move up and down the levels of humanity with ease.

The Man and I were finishing the store, and it was a big undertaking. I set up all of the bootleg equipment in the back so we could still take orders until the store got on its feet. I placed ads in the cool independent newspapers around town. I had membership cards made up. I bought the software to track everything. I was labeling and categorizing the whole library and all of the DVDs. The sign was put up, and stickers went on the door. A rubber corpse and a huge alien (in a hibernation tube!) hung high on the wall, looking down at us. I bought lava lamps, black lights and a huge TV. We had it all set up for the opening weekend.

I even paid a couple of chicks to dress up in latex outfits to walk around Ybor with signs, advertising it. One of them dressed as a devil and the other as a nun. One of their friends showed up just wearing a skanky latex dress. They went out with their signs. I opened the door to the store.

People scurried in and scurried out. Members joined, and others just bought DVDs or videos. It was a great night. The Man and I talked up our gore and cult films to no end. I had kung fu aficionados coming in to check my Hong Kong selection, and the indie film crowd were looking for certain long-lost gems. It felt great, and I was really happy.

As I was ready to lock the doors after the last customer, I realized the girls I hired to parade around Ybor were long overdue. I locked up the shop and went looking for them.

I walked down Main Street and found them halfway down. They were actually in a dark alley. One was puking on herself. One had a guy wrapped around her. And the other was just trashed, trying not to fall down. The signs were broken and covered with mud and dirt.

"What's going on? Are you guys okay?"

"Stephen! We walked down the street, and every bar and club pulled us in and made us dance on the bar and gave us free drinks!"

"So, how much advertising did you guys do with the signs?"

"We didn't do anything," the one said in between puking. "I need to go home."

I got the guy in the alley to agree to drive them home, and I followed in my car to make sure everyone made it safely. It was a really nice drive home, very satisfying.

A week after the opening, things went well. The Man and I were having fun. I tried to smoke occasionally with The Man, but I ended up paranoid and out of my mind. I'd never had this problem until after the night I met God. So I stopped smoking pot altogether. I missed it because I used to love to get baked and watch underground movies. It was a part of who I was. On the other hand, the experience of meeting God made me realize there is more to life. It also seemed that God had reprogrammed me to be a different person. Part of that reprogramming was that I couldn't smoke pot without getting paranoid.

Around this time, a good friend named Rhett came to my house. I knew him since the comic book store, and he's probably my best friend.

Rhett walked in and sat down on the same love seat Morpheus had used. It was normal bullshit talk at first: Work, girlfriends, and good times past.

Then he asked me a question that blew my mind.

"So, Steve, what made you listen to different songs, repeatedly, with the same visuals over and over again?"

I looked at Rhett. I had never told anyone that I would listen and watch the same music video—or the same movies—repeatedly in my quest to find the answers, then to find God.

"Wait! How do you know this?"

I'm used to going with the flow of things, but this came from left field. Rhett is a straight shooter, gave up drugs a long time ago. And I hadn't touched any LSD and/or nitrous for months (and it had been over a month since I'd used pot), so I'm as straight as can be.

I felt a door open. Slowly, but it opened all the same.

"I know, Rhett said. "And to be honest, a lot of people know what you did. You can't just go to the other side without certain people and entities finding out or even just feeling it."

I was dumbfounded.

"How do you know about the repeated—?"

"Because that's how you do it. The music and visual stimuli repeated over and over puts the mind into a hypnotic state. Since the mind isn't trying to find a new note or a new visual, it can take it all in by memory while you're experiencing it. It puts the user into a deep trance so his mind can pierce the actual fabric of this reality."

I didn't know what was going on since this was real, coming from a trusted (and straight) friend.

"I've never told you or anybody about what I was doing," I said.

"Stephen, I'm God!" he said, laughing and standing.

I was overjoyed. I stood up, and we hugged like long-lost brothers. I almost began to cry. In fact, I think I did.

Again, my mind was open to all possibilities, and here was one. My best friend turns out to be God, masquerading as a human. Nothing could be better.

I ran with the idea like a child with a brand new pair of sneakers.

"I've been looking all over for you," I said. "You can't imagine…"

"I think I can," he says laughingly.

We sit back down, and I said, "Do you mind if I ask you some questions?"

"Go ahead. I wouldn't have revealed myself to you if I wasn't ready to answer."

"What is going on?"

"I'm testing you."

"Why did you create us?"

"Boredom, experimenting, loneliness, fun."

"But there isn't much fun," I said. "War, poverty, desperation and sadness. I can go on."

"But there's also joy, happiness, peace, sex and love."

"But why the insanity of it all? Why aren't you here on earth?"

He said, "Because how can I really test souls? The mystery shows one's true character. I left laws behind that everyone knows."

"Like in the Bible. I just bought one to read."

"Oh? Why would you do that?"

I was perplexed. "To read the book you wrote?"

He said, "No, I didn't write that. Men wrote that using me as inspiration."

"So what are you trying to say?"

"You don't have to read it. It has good stuff in it, but view it more like Aesop's Fables or a Brothers Grimm fairy tale. Cautionary tales. Do you think Noah actually saved two of every creature and put them all on one continent and that the continents split less than 10,000 years ago and it wasn't written about? Do you think Jonah actually sat in the belly of a whale for three days? If the deadly plagues of Egypt actually happened with Moses, don't you think the Egyptians would have recorded such a massive event on the walls of the pyramids? Um, dinosaurs—hello?"

I said, "Well, I can agree, but…"

"No buts. It never says in the Bible you must believe it all."

"Okay. So what, then?"

"Everyone has a path in life, and if you don't choose to accept it, you won't move forward until your next life. And if you choose that path and stick to your virtues without falling into the abyss— which, by the way is way too easy, the longer your life goes on—you will be rewarded in the next life and move up to the next level."

"So you're saying reincarnation is real."

"You did experience that, didn't you?"

"Yes? But you should know that."

"So why doubt what I am saying?"

"It's more Hindu-based, even though everyone believes in a type of reincarnation."

"Exactly my point. Every Christian believes in reincarnation, otherwise you wouldn't be reborn into Heaven. There wouldn't be a second death and a second life. You took a lot of LSD and mixed it with nitrous and you went into a different reality while looking for God, did you not?"

"Yes."

"You've gone places only the holiest of people have even gone, and they have all reported back to those around them. Shame of it is, not many go as far as you have. You actually broke out of this reality and into the next. You reached the level of atrocity, the level of despair, and you pulled yourself up into the level of exhilaration. You found yourself with the powers of a god, and then you plunged into total isolation from humanity on the psychic plane of existence between life and death. You've been to the realms of the ether, and you're probably the most fucked-up of them all."

He continues, "It's usually holy men or women who stay away from society to cleanse themselves for such an adventure. Not you. I have to hand it to you: You shocked us all."

"So tell me something I need to know."

"Look at it this way, Stephen. If I close my eyes, I can see where everyone will be in 30 seconds from now. I can also see them ten years from now. I can even see them at the end of their life at the same time."

"So there is no free will?"

"I never said that. I just know where they will be. Look at it this way: If I throw up a deck of cards, I know where they will all land, and I know where every card will be."

"Well, if you know that, why have us live these lives all the way through? When babies are born, why not send them straight to their ultimate destinations right at that moment?"

"You're quick. But who says I'm not doing that already? You're going by your clock and the rotation of the sun and moon as your guide. That's not how I keep track of time. My time is limitless, and thirty seconds to me is a lifetime to all. Can you understand that?"

"Yeah, I can understand that."

"Good, now let me tell you what I want you to do: I want you to make a movie of this. Maybe even a book. A book to start and then a movie afterwards. That sounds good. I want you to lay off the drugs, quit smoking and be a better person. Learn to be humble, kind and understanding. And I want you to remember this always. Jesus, Mohammed and Buddha were all sons of God, and you are now too."

I was a little confused but listening to every word. It's not often you hear the secrets to the universe. Feeling comfortable, I began to ask other questions.

"What about black people? Why did you create them?"

"That was a mistake."

"What?"

"I didn't know that racism would cause such harm. The whole race thing was a total fuck up. I didn't think everyone would be so afraid of another skin color or attribute—or that people would blame whole societies for the woes of themselves for so long."

"Well, that's fucked up." I said. Then I asked, "What about avocados? Why are the pits so big?"

"Ah, another fuck up. But you knew that from George Burns' answer in *Oh God!*"

I laughed because he figured out my ruse. Before I could ask any more, God spasmed, and His eyes became glossy. Then one eye twitched, and suddenly my friend Rhett was back. He jumped up and said, "Dude! I gotta fucking leave!"

He ran for the front door. I tried to catch him.

"What the Hell is going on, Rhett? What's wrong?"

"I haven't had anything like that happen to me for years! I gotta fucking go!"

Rhett scrammed, and I closed the door. I laughed and lit a cigarette while my mind did cartwheels and gymnastics, trying to put more pieces of the puzzle together.

THE MUSE UNMASKED AND SATAN REVEALED

My reality began to collide with the other side. Nobody knew what I was doing but they were becoming a part of it. The other side began to take notice and use the people around me as pawns, showing me its reach. This reminded me that I am not alone and that there is more to life than what we can see around us.

I woke up the next day, exhilarated but confused. I got ready to work at the store as I thought about the night before.

After telling me he was God, my friend Rhett told me more universal secrets, but as the conversation progressed, I could hear the human vulnerability come out. I could hear God, but I could hear something else. Rhett's personality was coloring the words. And why did my friend freak out when our little interview was over? The Holy Ghost—or maybe even the unholy ghost—must have possessed my friend Rhett.

Feeling confident, I drove to the store. The Man was already there, working the cash register and watching a Japanese *Death File Black* on the huge-screen TV.

"Man, turn that off," I said. "If someone normal walks in the door, they're going to freak!"

He stopped the video and said, "Dude, I have to talk to you."

"Sure. What's up?"

He walked around the video aisle to stand in front of me. He pushed me, gently, on the shoulders and said, "Dude, I'm your muse!"

"What are you talking about?"

"I'm your personal muse, dude. I'm here to help you gain a deeper insight into your reality, bro! I'm here to guide you while giving you inspiration."

"Um, cool. Um, thanks?"

I didn't know what else to say. My friend's news of being my personal muse comes hot on the confusing heels of the Rhett/God incident, to say nothing of the hallucinatory events of the prior six months.

Muses are from Greek mythology, and they're usually women. Nine daughters of Zeus, not a guy who sold me drugs and who helped build my video store. By this time I had learned to always go with it, accept your fate and deal with the gods, demi-gods, muses and servants as they cross your path.

The Man-Muse continued: "Everyone on the other side has noticed you by now, dude. You can't do the shit you're doing without everyone noticing. You're not seeing the stop signs where normal people quit. You're not learning *some* answers and turning around. You're continuing down the highway, dealing with the mindfucks until you get the final answer."

"I've never told you about any of this," I said.

"How long have we been friends? Three, four years now? I was sent here for a reason and you know it. I've been in the background, as your friend. Helping you achieve what you want in life. Giving you the gumption, energy and wisdom to follow your dreams and helping you to make it a reality."

"Yeah, you have."

"No one saw you coming. No one expected a shit head like you to truly find or believe in what you're searching for. Better men than you have searched and given up."

The Man adjusted his Yankees baseball cap, smiled and continued: "Better men have turned around, found what they thought was their destination and took a different exit. Proclaiming it to be the truth. Men have made a living on less than what you have done. Some men have changed the world with far less than what you have accomplished."

It started to make sense to me.

"You sold me the acid I've been taking for the last year. So are you telling me this has all been a plan?"

The Man smiled and said, "So you understand what is happening to you! Even at this moment, I'm amazed, bro. We usually never tell people what we are or what we're doing. They normally can't comprehend it."

The Man returned behind the counter. His eyes fluttered a little, and he twitched ever so slightly.

The Man looked at me again and said, "Dude, where have I been? I don't even remember you coming in the front door."

"We just had a 30-minute conversation?"

"Weird. Well, I left off watching some killer shit! Dude, have you seen the Russian army soldier get his head stomped to the ground with a knife stuck in his throat and then get pulled in half?"

"Yeah, and it's disgusting."

"Oh, man, it's bad ass!"

"I try to not watch that shit anymore," I said. "It stays in the mind way too long."

"You've showed me the roughest shit on this earth, and now you don't want to see any more cool shit?"

"I got enough of that floating inside my head. I don't need it anymore."

The Man was obviously back to normal. I just stood there, letting everything take its course.

"That's cool," he said understandingly. "How about I take off since you're here now?"

When the door closed behind The Man, a chill ran down my spine as I stood alone in the store. The other side was now blaring into my reality. My mind raced.

Imagine for a moment that God was one of your friends. He does this to every soul. Imagine that every soul is actually surrounded by entities of Heaven and Hell. Think about one soul, surrounded by agents, twenty deep, of each camp. All of them manipulating and coercing the person to do good or bad, all different degrees and levels of sin or virtue.

This is what I found myself in. I must be breaking through if possession of friends was becoming a normal occurrence. It seemed the reality I once knew would be forever changed.

I ended up closing the store without a single person walking in the door. They dropped their videos in the slot box, but nobody came in to rent or even to say hello. My eBay account didn't sell, and neither did my website. It was as if I'd dropped off the face of the earth. It was probably a good thing, actually. It gave me the time to think.

On the drive home that night, I knew I had to open another door. Shit was too crazy now, and I needed to know more. I needed to find God in his own territory. I needed to know whether I was dealing with fake or false entities. I needed to know if I could trust my own mind and reality.

The road was a blur until I neared my house. After I pulled into the driveway, I walked up my sidewalk and said, "This is it. I'm going to find out everything."

At my front door, I fumbled for the keys. I found the right one and lifted it towards the doorknob.

The night of the day still shone as I prepared to open another door. I got the key ready and slid it gently into the keyhole. It sunk right in and hit the back of the lock. I turned it, and you could hear the tumblers slide into place.

As I slowly opened the door, multicolored flames shot out around the sides. With each new inch of opening, a multi-hued inferno increasingly engulfed the air around me. The apartment became a roaring blaze of hatred and desolation that I couldn't understand.

I wasn't afraid and I wasn't startled. By this time, I knew that everything that happened was supposed to happen. So I walked through the door and closed it behind me.

Every color of the spectrum shimmied to a different beat as the conflagration whispered and wavered to a life it never should have had. As I watched it undulate and flicker, I could somehow feel it all coming from my soul. It was as if each flame licked a different part of my psyche or sputtered from a different facet of me.

I was seeing the fires of Hell.

I was transfixed by its gaping maw, hypnotized until he came. It was the entity that was always there, always watching, always showing me things I thought I needed to know.

It rose from the flames and pulled itself into my realm. It stood there, staring at me and said, "Why are you back? You shouldn't be here!"

I said, "I need to know what is going on."

The fires wrapped all around me in another deep conflagration.

"You must kill yourself for your God!" it said.

It stared hatefully into my soul from the psychedelic flames. I looked back, petrified.

Its eyes blazed as colorless black holes that pulled my very essence to him. Its beard was wavering and changing. Its hair whipped around as if alive, and its face morphed into something I could see but couldn't understand.

I felt myself spasm internally. My personality broke like a huge mirror, and the living pieces all pulled themselves away from each other. It was as if every piece of my soul was a separate entity trying to claw out of the picture frame that was me.

It said again, "You must kill yourself for your God!"

My mind continued scattering. Every aspect of me ran in abnormal ways to get away. I could feel myself stripped of every personal characteristic and safeguard I had built from the beginning of my life. My soul was exposed.

My ego or any portion of my false personality was gone. I was truly alone. Whatever was left of me grasped onto what I knew or what I believed. Trying to figure it out, my mind latched onto the words that were said to me: "You must kill yourself for your God!"

Through my recent experiences, I had been conditioned to obey the wisdom of the entity, so I looked around for an object with which to kill myself. Luckily for me, I had no weapons. But as I did this, my mind kept turning around the entity's words.

"He didn't tell me to kill myself for him. He told me to kill myself for my God. For my God!"

My mind twisted as the flames burned all around me. My mind shouted, "Kill myself for my God!"

It came to me: "I thought this entity was my God. It had been showing me supposed truth. But my search for God had found a different god. One that knew it wasn't God but could masquerade as it. I've thought this was God, but it was something else."

I stood in the blazing inferno of this other dimension, surely the entranceway into Hell, and I stood firm. I knew suicide is an unpardonable sin, reasoning, "You'd have to change the plan of God to kill one's self while being forgiven at the same time. No one can receive forgiveness for self-murder, because you don't have any time after the act to ask for forgiveness. It must be the only act that can never be forgiven, because when you commit that sin, there is nothing after it."

Sure, as you lay there bleeding to death, you can ask for forgiveness, but you're still in the middle of taking the action. Once it's been fulfilled, you're dead.

My mind took hold of this little fact, and I looked into the Devil's eyes, and I told Him, "My God would never ask me to kill! My God would never tell me to kill myself. You're not my God! I can see through you for what you truly are!"

The entity wailed, twisted and turned as anger spewed from it like a whirling dervish.

My heart stopped. A sonic boom. This reality began to chase into itself. The inferno subsided and normalcy crawled back into my place. I saw the last of the multi-hued flames seep into crevices of everything. The burnt smell of my flesh and surroundings still floated all around me.

I found myself sitting on the couch. Empty balloons and Whip It cartridges were strewn about the living room floor. I clutched my head and began to cry, lost and alone again. All my work was for nothing! Everything I did got me closer to the Devil, not God.

But I began to think some more. And I had an epiphany that blasted me like a ton of bricks falling on my head.

"Okay, so I found you. The Devil, masquerading as God!" I yelled. "You showed me things, giving me some truth but twisting it to knock me off of the right path. You even possessed my friends, trying to confuse me. Then you told me to kill myself! A-ha! The Devil wouldn't do all this unless I was about to make a breakthrough!"

It made sense. The Devil wouldn't fuck with me so hard if I wasn't going down the right path. Maybe he wanted to confuse me into taking my own life, so I'd be just another soul, instead of the one who found ultimate truth.

I stood up and shouted, "Fuck you, Lucifer! Or whoever you may be! I'm still going to find God, and I am not going to fucking stop until I find out all of the answers, you fucking asshole!"

I flopped back onto the couch, and a smile crossed my face. I could feel all the pieces of my ego crawl back into my personality, trying to shield me. I knew I'd just passed a test and my soul began to sing.

My extreme joy in that moment cannot fully be conveyed. But it should be enjoyed nonetheless as a battle we have both won: I can pass this information along to you because I am still alive.

As my laughter died down, I reached for the remote control to get my mind off of this episode. The remote control lay on top of the Holy Bible I'd bought a week ago. It hadn't been opened and hadn't been read. Little did I know the importance and devastation that book would bring me. I didn't know at that time that a mortal couldn't go to Hell and back without one.

MONKS VISIT THE STORE AND A RUNAWAY CHILD FINDS HIS PLACE

We both find ourselves in the familiar library. I'm drinking, and so are you. The fire is roaring while the books are warping, but neither of us care now.

I cover my face, afraid to continue. But I have to. The seat you're sitting in is hotter than it should be, so you readjust yourself.

You can tell I'm tortured and confused. But you actually see a certain added sense to the events, because you're an outside observer.

You tell me, "Don't worry. It makes more sense than you know. I need you to continue and tell me the rest."

I lift my head and try to look at you when shame crosses my face. I say, "You don't understand. What if I really destroyed Heaven? Was I following the Devil and being manipulated with half-truths and lies? Was this the Devil reeling in my soul to make me an Antichrist?"

"But you've said this is just the beginning of wisdom and that there is redemption. You also say you have been saved and you know God. I believe in that now."

I look up at you, tears streaming from my eyes, and I say, "Thank you for listening to me. I'm sorry I get lost sometimes. There's just so much that a human can bear."

I wipe the tears from my eyes.

* * *

This is where the testimony gets a little weird.

My life had taken a turn into the Twilight Zone, and I didn't know how to get back. My ruby slippers didn't work, and my time machine had a dead battery.

I left for work and arrived at the store early. I opened the shop and stuck in a kung fu video to watch. The movie was called *Eastern Condors*, starring Sammo

Hung, and it was a Hong Kong-made *Rambo* knock-off with a group of Chinese soldiers instead of just one. Explosions, death, and murder during the Vietnam War on the Asian side. I just enjoyed the heroism and crazy kung fu action.

I was watching this movie when I saw a gaggle of cloaked people stop in front of my store. Eight people wore what looked like monks' clothes and seemed to pray at my front door. After a moment, they were leaving.

This isn't a normal situation that happens at my store, so I jumped out of my chair and ran to the front door. I stuck my head outside, looking down the street and yelled, "Hey! What were you guys doing?"

The monks stopped in their tracks. Several of them looked back at me and the others refused to lift their heads. One monk, the main one, turned around defiantly. Looking me straight in the eyes, he said, "We were praying over your store. We find it in league with the Devil. We do this to all of the clubs and bars in Ybor City."

"No, no, no," I said with a laugh. "I'm not in league with the Devil! Come back here and let's talk."

They looked at each other, then back at me.

"C'mon, c'mon. I'm not going to bite, even if you think I am. I like it that you prayed over my store. No one has ever done that for me."

The monks walked back towards my store, then stopped and said, "We can't come in. This is a place of Satan."

"I couldn't have this store if it wasn't for God. God knows everything and I wouldn't be able to be here if it wasn't for Him."

They came closer to the front door, and I walked out, closing the door behind me.

"Why exactly were you praying over my store?"

The main monk answered for the group. "Well, you have the word 'cult' on your window and your phone number uses three sixes. And it's called Video Mayhem, with 'mayhem' meaning chaos and destruction. Your store has symbols and words that tell us you are following Satan."

I laughed, and they all looked up at me. It was interesting because they were all about 5'2". I wouldn't normally mention this, but I've never had so many small men around me, much less in hooded cloaks.

"The word 'cult,' in the movie business, just means a movie people watch over and over again. Have you ever watched a movie more than three times?"

They all nod their heads yes.

"That's all that means—a film people watch over and over again. Now, my phone number has three sixes in it, but it's actually 4,666. It's not actually 666. Most people refuse to have this number or any number that has 666 in it. I took it because nobody else wanted it, and I figured it would be easy to remember."

I felt petty for defending this stuff, so I shifted gears.

"Do you know how much I talk to my customers about God?"

111

"Really?"

"Listen, I only sell horror flicks, kung fu flicks and anime in this store. Most of my films have to do with the darker side of life. A lot even have to deal with the Devil. How can a person not be exposed to the realities of the Devil and God in their personal life? Most of my customers don't go to church. If they watch a movie about possession or demons, then how can they not think about it? How can they not say, 'what if?'"

The main monk looked me in the eyes, and he could feel the warmth in them. He opened up to me.

"We have been praying over these bars and stores in Ybor. We usually get kicked out or threatened, pushed away. We have never had an owner invite us in and talk about what we found offensive."

"Never?" I said.

"They see us pray in front of their stores or clubs and bars and become violent and call us names. It's so disheartening sometimes."

The monks whisper amongst themselves, and then I'm told, "You have blessed us with understanding. You have explained to us what we found frightening. We truly didn't understand. We would never have comprehended that you are a soldier of God and you are reaching out to those in need."

My smile stretched from ear to ear.

"You see those two chairs, in the front of my store," I asked. "Right in the front window?" I point to the two little chairs at the front of the store with a little table between them. "I use those to talk to many customers about life, love, and God."

The monks are at ease but have to leave.

"Please come back," I said, "because I would love to talk to you more."

"We will."

They said another prayer—hopefully a different one this time, as I was no longer Hellspawn in their eyes. Then they turned around and walked down the strip to pray over the rest of the ungodly folk.

I returned inside and giggled as I rewound *Eastern Condors*. I began to hope they would come around and talk to me so I could understand more. They did. Every day, for over a month, they came to my store, prayed over my shop and me. I began to give them money like I did the homeless people in the streets of Ybor. We became friends. I learned a house was given to the Catholic Church in Ybor City and that the Monks, learning the ins and outs of their religion, lived there.

I don't like Catholicism but can't refuse someone who believes in God, even if I find something wrong in the theology. In the long run, they knew about God more than I so I listened and listened hard.

All of these monks who prayed over the iniquities of the flesh were battling their own iniquities. Almost all of them were gay, and I mean that honestly.

You know gay people when you come across them. I don't mean anything pejorative. Who cares if you're gay or not. Well, they certainly did, and that was exactly the problem for them. In the Catholic Church, being gay is a choice and a big sin. These men just couldn't live a life outside the church because then they would be gay. The only place they could hide from the sins of the flesh was in a celibate, hood-wearing monastic order.

I know Protestant pastors don't have to be celibate to minister to people. Celibacy is not a requirement in the Bible as far as I know. I think men of the cloth should be married so they can see the real love that God gave us. Being in love is the most amazing thing we can ever experience.

In any case, I felt sorry for the monks that became my friends, so I tried to help them. I found they had a shelter right next to their house. They told me they were teaching homeless kids and used videos to help in the process. I found out they had a twelve-inch B&W TV to teach over 20 homeless kids how to spell and count. Once they told me that, I gave them my four-foot wide big-screen TV in the hopes the kids could finally read their spelling and counting lessons.

I had a soft heart and gave change often. I welcomed some of the homeless into my shop so we could watch movies or talk. I had my car broken into and my stereo boosted because they knew I wouldn't call the cops on them.

Yeah, I've been ripped off, lied to, condemned, and prayed over. I've been manipulated, stolen from, and abused more times than I want to remember. I've actually been drugged in a bar by total strangers and prevented things from getting worse by leaving and managing to get to my store before the roofies kicked in. Ah, the life of a shop owner in Ybor City.

Around this time, I talked about God with many people. I never argued with anyone. I just told them about the hope I had for Him and that they too would one day reach out to Him to try to make sense of this mess called life. I had told people I met God, but I changed that to say I met the Devil or, sometimes, even one of his lesser minions.

Around this time, one of my customers came in right at closing time. Let's call him Jack. Jack was about my age, around 34 years old. His complexion was a little pale and he was red around the edges due to his fair color. He liked horror movies and kung fu. That's really all I knew of Jack. We rarely spoke, and he only came in once a month, so I was quite surprised at the invite he sprang on me.

"Steve! Let's go get a beer together."

"Thanks, Jack, but I was going to go home tonight and take it easy. It's a really long drive."

"Well, I think you're going to want to. Want to know why?"

"I'm really busy, Jack, and I just want to…"

"I'm an Antichrist, Steve, and I was sent to talk to you."

A shiver ran up my back. Hairs stood up.

Jack laughed and said, "I knew that would get your attention. You definitely got our attention. I can say that much for you."

Shock turned to a mild understanding. I told him, "I'll be right with you. Never had a beer with an Antichrist before."

"You wouldn't believe how many times you have talked with an Antichrist, or even an Angel for that matter. I'll be waiting outside."

I quickly put the money in the safe and closed the store while thinking about what this could mean. Was I dead and about to go to Hell? Was I living these last couple of months in limbo or purgatory, on the way to either Heaven or Hell?

I'd never talked to Jack about anything I went through so this wasn't a trick. This was happening in normal reality and not psychedelic reality because it had been over 6 months since my last confrontation with the Devil.

I stepped outside, ready to go to Hell, and locked the door behind me. Jack said, "Let's hit the outside bar, close by. We can talk, smoke, and drink there."

We walked towards the closest outside bar. Jack spoke.

"I notice you're still smoking. Thought you were trying to quit."

"I am. Addiction is a bitch. It's on again, off again. Gum doesn't work too well anymore. I end up with the hiccups."

"I take it The Big Guy Upstairs told you to stop, huh?"

"Yeah, told me to stop a lot of stuff."

"How's that going for you now?"

"The drugs have been the easy part so far. Pot makes me go out of my mind. Sometimes I'm talked into doing some ecstasy, but it turns into Hell itself. It's hard to lose friends when that was all you had in common."

"Yeah, He does that to certain people," Jack said. "Too bad He did it to you. You would have been a great Antichrist."

I was floored. I didn't say anything else until the bar. I ordered an Amberbock and he ordered a Budweiser. I sipped my beer, relishing it because I didn't know if this was going to be my last beer before being reaped down to the bowels of Hell.

At this time, I knew things weren't always as they seemed. I came to the conclusion that both God and the Devil were working on people unaware. Others knew and fought every moment to either do what was right or what was wrong.

I also believed that if the Devil was to come for me in a crowded room and set my soul afire in front of thousands, I could burn to ashes and float to Hell and nobody would know or remember that it happened. I was in God's Twilight Zone, and I was in another episode that could go anywhere.

"Okay, why does an Antichrist want to have a beer with me?"

"It looks like you have been taking trips to the other side, and everyone has noticed. You've created quite the ripple outside the plane of existence we pretend to be in. Some of us thought it was time for you to hear our feelings on the matter."

"Who's us?" I asked.

"That's beside the point. I'm not going to ask you what you learned on the other side. I don't want you to poison my beliefs. I will ask you this, though: What and who did you meet?"

I take a huge pull off of my beer and I set it down and began telling him:

I thought I was meeting God. I began learning knowledge and wisdom that was hidden from normal men. I found the philosopher's stone and used it to learn and to find God but I found something else that was masquerading as God. Some of the truths were still truths but they were mingled in with lies. That way, when I learned some truth, it made the lies go down easier.

Jack laughed, but his eyes trembled as he said, "So you met Him didn't you? You met the Father of all Lies and you're still here. You're still a-fucking-live."

He continued, "Wow, not many men have ever done that—lived to tell the tale. Not get lost in the lies that He disguised with truth. You're in his book now, you know."

A shudder rippled through me and settled in my brain.

"Don't worry. Well, be worried a little. You're not in the Book of the Damned. You're in the book of souls he's lost, personally lost. So congratulations, Stephen. You're probably on the front page of that book now."

I said, "Why would...?"

"You don't understand what you were up against. The Father of all Lies, He who Masquerades as an Angel of Light, The Liar, The Deceiver of all Mankind."

I said, "And now I'm talking to an Antichrist."

He said, "Exactly. I don't think you realize who you are supposed to be, do you?"

I shook my head no.

"So, you searched for God and found the Devil instead. Do you know how to make a difference in the world? Do you know or understand how to get your word out to mankind?"

I said, "Be a rock star, an actor, or even a politician."

Jack laughed and said, "You're exactly right. If you get enough people to follow you, then they will believe in what you say. They will do what you say. They will even pay you to tell them what to do."

"I don't want that," I said.

"Then you can write a book. How's that sound?"

"That sounds better because I don't want to become a false idol to people."

Jack laughed and said, "Oh, you will though. You were given a vision, I'm sure—one of your future?"

"That's not going to happen," I retorted. "That was a possible vision if I followed the Father of Lies. And if I write a book, it's not going to be a "follow me and here're the answers to everything" book. I'm going to write it from my heart and as humbly as I can."

"You're quick, Stephen. No wonder He wanted you enough to make a personal visitation. I have a proposal for you, but before I say it, I have to ask: How many times did He visit you?"

I took another drink. "Twelve to fifteen times, maybe more. This might be another encounter right now. He could be hiding behind your eyes as we speak, Antichrist."

Jack stood up. "You're kidding me. He tried to seduce you that many times? The Father of Lies doesn't take his time on just normal everyday souls, especially if they're in his camp already."

Jack chugged his beer as if something was wrong.

"You're wanted by us, you realize that, right? What was your future vision about?" he asked.

"I'm not going to tell you because it hasn't happened yet. I'm not going to let it happen."

"It must have been a doozy. What if it was already in place and you couldn't stop it because it was already foretold?"

"Then that means there is no free will, and I believe we have it."

"The Book of Life has already been written, and those that are damned and those that are saved are already recorded. You don't know who you are, do you?"

"I'm nobody but a follower of God," I said.

"That's the spirit! I wish I had a camera. No one is going to believe I met you later."

"Now you're just being creepy," I said.

He slammed his beer down and said, "Here's my proposal to you. I'll make sure you get a million dollars if you act against a belief right now."

"What?"

He said, "You heard me. I will make sure you get a million dollars if you act against a belief right now. You'll have the money in less than a month's time. But the catch is: You will never, ever fall asleep again because you acted against your belief."

"A million dollars would be nice, but c'mon. I'm not going to let a self-described Antichrist tempt me to act against a belief for money. And I'll never sleep again? That's ridiculous. The answer is no."

Jack said, "Easy money, man."

"No. Now tell me: If you're a self-professed Antichrist, what is your take on God? I'm curious."

Jack's eyes and demeanor changed then and became sporadic and twitchy. As if whatever he had in him was gone and I was left with plain ol' Jack. He told me his god was the government and that it's telling us what we have to do; we tithe to it via taxes, and it has no place in telling us what we can and should do. I listened to his ramblings for a few minutes and excused myself with no real pleasantries. I never saw him again at my video store. I guess he did what he had to do.

During the long drive home, my mind replayed the offer: A million dollars to act against a belief, and I would never sleep again. I didn't realize it at the time, but it was going to be rough night.

I got home and made myself comfortable. I actually forgot what the offense was. Maybe I watched a dirty movie, or I looked at someone with lust, or I lied to someone or did something even worse. All I do remember is I did act against a belief that night.

I lay down to go to sleep, and panic flooded my mind. My heart beat out of its chest, and I sweated profusely. My mind kept echoing that Antichrist's wager about acting against a belief, especially the part about not sleeping again. I prayed to God in remorse, but I still tossed and turned in an all-night panic attack. I didn't fall asleep at all. I groggily showered and dressed and headed to work.

The Man and I parted ways around this time. Since I no longer got high, we couldn't easily hang out. Our roads were two different paths; he even said this to me. I really appreciated the hard work he did to make the store a reality, and I thanked him from the bottom of my heart.

Around the time I was visited by an Antichrist, I had another unusual visitor at my store. It was late, around 8 p.m., when a kid walked in. He was about 14. He looked around, and I noticed his young age.

"Hey, how old are you?"

He told me.

"You can't be in here," I said. "The store is Rated R because we have some disgusting and adult-themed movies in here. You gotta go!"

"I have no place to go. I ran away from home."

I walked up to him and said, "Where are you running away to?"

He said, "Here."

"Here? My video store?"

He told me, "Yeah, my friends told me you were a good guy and really cool to talk to about anything, so I wanted to go to someplace where I wouldn't be judged."

Wow. I wasn't expecting anything like this. I turned off the TV, and I motioned for him to sit in the chairs at the front of the store. He told me he was living with his grandparents and was sick and tired of being told what to do. We talked about school and how he didn't want to attend anymore. He was upset at his parents for abandoning him and because his grandparents were mean, giving him curfews and chores.

I told him his grandparents loved him and were just showing him how life is. The chores are just like work when you're older. I asked him if his grandparents loved him, and he said, "Yes." I told him, "Great, just remember that. Life is hard, really hard."

Then he said he wanted to do what I was doing and have a cool movie store. I told him, "It's not as awesome as it seems. It's a lot of hard work."

I do believe we talked about God for a second, and he believed and went to church with his grandparents, so that was great. My mind went to ease with that aspect. I needed a cigarette at the time and I asked him to come outside with me so we could continue to talk.

He asked me about cigarettes, and I told him, "I have been trying to quit because it's an addiction. It's something that my body is forced to do and that my mind has been programmed to do. It's very hard, and it's one of the stupidest things I have ever done in my life. It might seem like it's cool when you're young, but you become a slave to it. You don't want to become a slave to anything, do you?"

"No, I just thought it was cool."

I said, "It's not. It's the worst thing you can do to yourself. I'm not as cool as you think I am."

He said, "I won't smoke. I don't want to be a slave to anything."

I began to tell him, how he should stay in school, even go to college. I talked to him about the wonders of education and how he should learn about everything he can, because the more you learn, the smarter you are, and the smarter you are, the better you will be in life.

He agreed because for some odd reason, he respected me. Sitting on the curb, I gave him a metaphor for life.

"Imagine your life is a big canvas. Picture it in your mind and think about the beginning of your painting of life. You're fourteen years old, and you are lucky if you have one seventh of it painted."

I stood and showed him an imaginary frame. I showed him how little of the painting had been painted by his living up to that exact moment.

"Now imagine the rest of the canvas is totally empty. Every day you live, and every month and every year, means another inch that is painted on that canvas."

"You're going to be painting this empty canvas with your life and when you get to the end of it, what is that painting going to look like?"

He said, "I want it to look good, like I accomplished stuff and made a difference."

"That would be a beautiful picture, son. I would love to see it someday."

My heart felt very light and my soul beamed with happiness.

"So, how about we call your grandparents? I'm sure they're worried about you."

He said, "Okay."

The grandparents had had no clue where he went and were so relieved. They told me he would talk about the store and wanted to go when he turned seventeen. They never expected him to show up there now. I told them about our talk.

They were a little bit taken aback; I had made headway with their grandson in a cult video store.

When they picked him up, I said, "Hey, remember what I said, okay?"

He said, "Yeah, keep painting the picture I want to leave behind."

I laughed and said, "Never forget about that picture. Sometimes you might not see it, but someday you will."

I closed up the shop and prayed I made a difference in his life. I know he made a difference in mine.

I have never been able to remember that kid's name. I used it a number of times as we spoke, but as soon as he left the store, it disappeared from my memory.

I know what you're thinking and so am I. He might have been another test or maybe even an angel. The innocence and the wonder of it all takes my breath away. A 14-year-old boy was at his wit's end, ran away, came to my store and talked to me because I wouldn't judge him.

That night, I slept the sleep of reason. For a while, I worked and played and didn't think much of the metaphysical world.

Then one night, I slipped into bed and lay there, waiting for the soft envelope of sleep to overtake me. But it didn't. Something was amiss. Something bubbled up into my subconscious and took hold. I didn't know where it was going, but I felt it for what it was. My prayers—or possibly my nightmares—were about to be answered

THE LORD ANSWERS THE CALL AND THE BIBLE SPEAKS

We find ourselves in the library again, but it's different this time. Each book on each shelf is switching and spreading out like a piece of silly putty. Nothing can be sharply discerned except for the two of us. You look at the ceiling and the floor, and they're not just breathing, they're hyperventilating. The fire's flames burn backwards. Hypno-condusive flames eat into each other instead of burning outward. The leather on your chair flows slowly, and you feel it spread down the body of the chair but still keep its form. You slide to the end of the chair and wiggle your ass back onto it. You see me trying to hold it together for both of our sakes. You look into my soul and find an unseen level of fear.

Onyx spikes thrust from every inch of space around us. They stab the air, making their way towards us. You realize that I lost control of our library setting. I clutch my face in desperation. The sobs of my soul wrack my body to the hilt.

"Stephen, I've seen where you have been, and I know what you need to do. Please, control your mind while I am here."

I try to hold back the terrors of what I witnessed. I gasp and almost fall over. But you're here, giving me the support I didn't have before.

The onyx spikes suddenly stop about a foot away from us. You look around and see them wrapped around the whole room, ready to eradicate us. My tears continue, but I lean up and wipe the sadness from my eyes. I look and actually see you for who you are.

I feel your pain and torture, your happiness and joy, and I can understand more than anyone else. But in turn, I know you feel my fury and suffering. I know you can understand my exhilaration and ecstasy. I know you're a soul wanting the answers. I'm just afraid to follow through.

The spikes melt onto the floor. I regain control of our surroundings, and you feel it. The fire burns like a fire while the melted spikes wash down the drain.

I laugh and say, "Good thing you imagined that drain earlier. I wouldn't have thought about it earlier, but that's how everything happens."

I stand and continue, "I'm sorry for letting it get out of control for us. I never wanted to, and I didn't think it would. Again, I'm sorry."

I pace back and forth, in front of the fireplace, and say, "I brought you to places that probably should have been off limits. But I thought it would be easier for you to understand."

You shift in the chair, uncomfortable.

I'm still pacing. I say, "I'm about to meet my Maker and go into the bowels of Hell. You can't come with me."

Your hands shudder as you grasp what I am saying.

I say, "You can't come."

The library is perfectly still, and you could read everything around you. But you're staring at me. You know this is it. No turning back.

I lean towards you and say, "I'm sorry. What I'm about to experience is only for me. I'm going to leave you on this level, and I am going forth into what the Lord wants me to. Think of it this way: I'm a deep sea diver, and you're on the boat. We have an intercom, and I'll be in constant contact. But I'm at the mercy of what I encounter. Nothing you can do will change my outcome."

You don't know what is going to happen, but you know I'm about to say goodbye. We lock gazes and make up our minds to do what is right.

"I don't remember everything I experienced in Hell but I will try. The deeper I went, the more confusing it became. I hope you don't mind. I didn't take any notes as I did for everything else."

I breathe hard, and an electrostatic door opens in between us. The static electricity of it makes our hair stand on end. I lean around the door and say to you, "I wouldn't be going back or even try to remember what happened to me. But it will always be here in my mind."

The door shifts and pulsates in front of me. It caves in parts towards me, and hands, forming themselves out of the static, grab me. They clutch my hands and ankles while trying to thrust me into the entryway.

I scream. The last door of my life pulls me through.

* * *

I find myself lying in bed, trying to sleep.

I felt something approaching but didn't know what it was. My body tingled. I tried to roll over and go to sleep, but a dread came over me. Every cell in my body resonated with a low-pitched hum that gently shook me. It was like 1,000 monks all humming the same song in my head. I felt a presence of unknown power coming closer and closer.

That's when the room started to glow. It grew whiter with each second that flew by in my primitive mind. It culminated in a flash that grabbed my soul.

The rumble started deep within me, as if I finally knew where my soul was. It grabbed hold of my soul and shook it, slowly at first, but growing increasingly stronger. It was as if the judgment of God manifested itself in me and wouldn't let go until I knew.

That's when I realized I was gone, in a full-blown seizure. Every inch of me was seizing, and nothing—not an inch of me—was mine. Not a single atom of my body was in my control, and the Fear of God crept out of my soul and into my whole being. The whole bed shook as my body created a fever pitch of unrelenting spasms that were merciless. The Lord began to take hold.

I tore into spastic fits that could be mistaken for a fucking earthquake. I knew the Lord was visiting me, and I looked around the room, wondering what to do. There was nothing I could do. Absolutely nothing, as in life and in death. All we can do is go with the flow, whether up or down, side to side, or Heaven or Hell. We are nothing but actual amoebas that are tossed and thrown away in our deaths. We have no say in the matters of our afterlife.

The popcorn ceiling began dripping towards the floor. All my acid trips made the popcorn move like a wave on the ocean, but it had never dripped to the carpet. Thousands of nodules from the ceiling stretched and seeped in an amazing display of profundity that overtook me as my Lord moved closer to me.

But it wasn't done in a loving way. This was a Fear of God that seemed to say I was a fucked-up human being who should never have dared to try to find Him.

I was finally getting a taste of—or even an actual nod from—the Lord, that he took my search and my quest as an actual desperate plea for His knowledge, His forgiveness, and an answer for life that I needed. I was willing to die for Him, in exchange for finding out what is actually real, in His eyes.

Otherwise, I don't think He would have given me an audience.

This was between me and the Principalities and The Lord. The room spun, and I was tossing to and fro. I had never experienced anything like this, and I pray I never will again.

I crawled out of bed, still in a full-blown seizure. I knew in my soul that I needed one thing and one thing only. The brand new Bible I had bought was sitting in the living room. It had never been opened or read.

Something inside told me I needed it. Whether it was my soul, The Lord, or even my personal Angels. I knew I needed it. I stood up, my legs shaking and my body trembling in a full-blown fit. I staggered out of the room, trying desperately to find my Book.

If you have never been in a full-blown seizure, this is how it can be best expressed: Your body is not your own. You want to control part of your body—say, a muscle or a ligament—but you can't. There's nothing you can do to stop your body from malfunctioning. Your mind is locked within your body, and you're dealing with a breakdown between mind and body. While your thoughts and feelings race inside you, your body is at a total loss. You lose all hope.

I could barely walk, but I managed to make it to my living room, looking for my Bible. It was on the coffee table, where I'd left it. I grabbed it without thinking twice, and I began to struggle back to my bed.

All my muscles still working against me, I flopped down on my bed like a fish out of water, shaking and spazzing uncontrollably. I laid there, begging God for relief and for the knowledge I'd been searching for this whole time. I wanted a deep connection with my God, to make life right and to please him in everything I did.

As my body flailed and shook, my mind was either given an idea or came up with it independently: Let the Bible open up, by itself, of its own accord.

I let my new Bible open up for me.

My spasms began to subside as the book opened. I held it in front of me, and my body became its old self again. The seizure stopped, and I looked at the Bible, and there it was:

It was opened to the Ten Commandments. I was amazed and in total awe as the Lord showed me exactly what I needed to hear from him.

I began to feel a calming effect and a peace I had never felt before in my life. I felt it in my soul and knew what I had to do. So I began to read the words of the Ten Commandments and take them to heart.

I read those words in less than five minutes, and I closed the Holy Book and felt good for myself.

That's when the world began to shake again, and I began to spasm and seize, harder than before. I clutched the Bible and figured I mustn't have taken the Commandments to heart.

Perhaps I didn't think about them hard enough, covering my whole life, reviewing what I have done to break them all in every minute and every moment of my life.

So I opened it with my hands holding the back and front covers, letting it truly open to where it may, letting the Holy Bible guide me towards what I needed to know. It opened back up to the Ten Commandments.

The Bible had never been read before this, so it had neither earmarks nor a single creased page. I was seizing and spazzing, and knew I was in God's realm.

The spasms died down, and my body became my own again as I re-read the Ten Commandments. This time, as every Commandment was read, I looked through my life and realized how I had broken them all.

I took each Commandment as directed specifically towards me. I thought about them. And I asked for the forgiveness of each sin I'd committed against God.

My body was my own again, but I also found a peace I have never known before. There I was in front of The Lord, who had shown Himself to me. Not because I was a sinner, not because I was Holy, but because He knew I needed Him.

Yes, I had used drugs in my quest, but not this time. I was as straight as a lamb. I think He took pity on me because I was surrounded by evil in its many guises and still looked up to Him while all of those around me didn't want anything to do with Him! This is a quote from my Bible that I know in my heart of hearts had an actual bearing on my journey!

Matthew 7 :7-12. "Ask and it will be given to you; seek and you will find; knock and the door will be opened to you. 8. For everyone who asks receives; the one who seeks finds; and to the one who knocks, the door will be opened."

The door was finally opened, and I came to the last of the Commandments, with my very life hanging in the balance. I finished the sins of my life up until that point, and I exhaled my deepest sigh of relief. I closed the book and laid it on my chest and began to breathe the breath of the saved.

My room slowly whitened, and I felt my body tremble again. I cried aloud, "Lord, please stop! What am I supposed to do now?"

I could feel It, His presence. He told me to let the Bible open by itself again. Trembling, I let it open up.

It opened to Proverbs, and thus was The Beginning of Knowledge by starting with the Fear of the Lord. I read Proverbs as if the Lord was actually talking to me from within. I was no longer trembling, and I finally learned what the Lord wanted me to know. I read and I read some more until I was at a place I knew I should stop. So I did. I laid the Bible on my chest because I felt something else.

My heart began to beat again, and I felt the forgiveness of the Lord. But my spirit began to quicken. My body began to shift as I began the next leg of my journey.

I wasn't prepared for this. I didn't need to know what was on the other side any longer. But my body tensed up and my eyes began to roll into the back of my head as the Lord began to push me beyond the realms of reality into something no man is ever ready for.

No man wants to see the inner workings of the Lord, much less this. I didn't know why I was being thrust down there. I knew I had been begging for it, but just because I had doesn't mean I was ready.

I could feel it well up and push me down. I began to fight it, but you can't fight what the Lord wants you to see; you're going to see it.

My body quivered and shook as darkness enveloped me. The bed began to spread its mattress around me, and darkness coated the other side. I prayed to the Lord. My body began to fall to a depth I couldn't fathom.

I felt myself falling at the terminal velocity of death. I dropped like a bullet being shot out of a gun, leaving this earth and heading towards something I never wanted to see. My free fall had a purpose, and it took me straight to Hell.

THE FALL INTO HELL, DEMONIC DRUGS, AND THE MOUNTAINS OF GREED

I fell into utter blackness.

I'm not talking about the blackness that occurs when you close your eyes and you see light on the other side of your eyelids or even closing your eyes and seeing what seems like electricity. I'm talking about complete and absolute darkness that swept over me like a plague. Nothing encased in nothingness is the only way I can explain it.

I gained momentum as I fell, desperately wanting to hit rock bottom. Time and space had no meaning during the fall. I lost everything and was just pure experience. There was nothing left of my personality. It was just pure terror and utter fear of meeting my own damnation that I had brought onto myself. That's when I hit.

I slammed to the ground and immediately felt like a prisoner encased in Hell, which is exactly where I was and what I was. I landed face first, and I laid there for a second until a cacophony began ringing all around me. It wasn't like what you would expect of Hell; it was more of a pulsation, a constant sound and energy that emanated from everything.

I'm going to try to explain every detail I experienced in a way that you can understand it. So you can feel it and actually picture it within your mind's eye. This sound or energy was all purveying and drenched everything in its nature.

When you take a hit of pot (or take drugs, or pills, or even drink), you get a "buzz", or you "alter your mindset." The buzz you get from altering your mind on Earth, while still alive, is totally different than the feeling or "buzz" you feel in Hell.

The buzz you get on pot is nice and high, almost like a really high keynote on the musical scale. Alcohol is a little lower, a couple octaves below the pot high. But the cocaine buzz is a couple octaves higher than the pot high, but it moves up and down, like a sliding scale while you're on it. Nitrous Oxide is a lot

126

higher in the scale than pot, and that's why it can knock you out—a matter of how the internal pitch of the drug interacts with your brain.

The mind-altering substances that produce a sound may change slightly and waver some, but mostly they stay the same frequency until you come down. I know about the mind's internal audio signals; they will alter your perception (writing this may get someone to actually document it).

I'm giving you this example so you can truly understand the pounding awfulness of the sound inside one's mind when in Hell. It was the lowest key in the scale, and it flowed into itself and through you like a divining rod that knew and spoke to you in terror.

I had only laid there for three seconds when the energy of Hell engulfed me. It felt like an eternity as I tried to regain my senses. I opened my eyes and saw myself lying on the hard unrepentant ground. No bushes, plants or trees; it seemed like a marble surface that spread everywhere.

I suddenly heard the voices of two creatures. One screamed, "There's another one! Grab him!"

I was tackled even though already down. They flipped me over so I was facing what should have been the sky but wasn't; there was just emptiness. The two men were reptilian in nature, and they were screaming in my face as if I were the last person on earth.

"You need to take this! You need some of this!"

The first reptilian demonoid spat in my face with the contempt and disgust of what he was actually doing. The second demonoid stuck his face into my own and screamed, "You fucking have to do this!"

Their knees pressed onto my chest as they—still screaming—pulled out huge hypodermic needles. I was desperate to scream but had no voice. It was lost, just as I lost my fear in the fall. I was ready to accept everything that happened to me. I accepted my fate and was ready for the Damnation of Hell.

I saw a disgusting green fluid oozing from the hypodermics, and then I noticed the needle had barbs on it. I tried to struggle, but acknowledgment of your place in Hell tends to make a soul accept what it thinks it deserves.

They continued screaming at me, wanting me to do the drugs, wanting to shove them in me. I stared at them in absolute dread. Their skin was embedded with reptilian scales, slit pupils and snake-forked tongues. Their ears were somewhat folded into their heads, and their voices continued echoing in my mind, each word overlapping another but I could understand them. When I had taken in the full horror of it all, that's when they looked at each other and said, "He said YES!, He said YES!"

I shook my head "No." I tried to say, "No." But I couldn't. Nothing came out, not even a whimper.

127

That's when they both grabbed my arms and, without even trying to find a vein, slammed the needles into both my arms! They hit the plungers, and the green gook flowed into my body.

I can only liken it to a dog taking what is given to it from its master because it knows its place. That's not how I thought I acted, but that's exactly what happened.

They ripped the needles out of my skin and laughed to each other as my head began to swim with the effects of the mysterious green ooze. They both jumped off me, laughing and carousing as if this was their first time for this. Then one of them said, "He's different, you know."

But the other promptly yelled, "There's another one over there!"

He pointed into the distance and ran in that direction, his diabolic companion following. I shook, convulsed, and spewed from my mouth the same colored junk they had shot me up with. I tried to get my bearings as the sound of Hell pulsed through my body. My head swimming, I dragged myself to my feet. I stumbled but regained my footing, and I looked over the expanse around me. An unending scene of despair and torment shook me as I realized where I was and what I had lost.

I was in Hell, and I couldn't comprehend why, but my life had led me to its finality, and I accepted it.

I stumbled forward, not knowing where I was going, but I needed to go there, wherever it was. The sound of Hell just dampened every part of me, and I didn't care what was going on, but I had to reach where I was going. There wasn't an expanse of fire, just an unending torrent of rocks and canyons that jutted and beckoned everywhere. I tripped, fell and stumbled on everything in my path until I got where I was going.

My mind was reeling about what I had just experienced with the reptilians, since it wasn't a "seven deadly sins" scenario, but rather a peer-pressure thing. My mind grasped the fact that peer pressure can be a sin and that talking a person into something against their better judgment can be a sin.

That thought grabbed me by the soul and held it for all its worth when a ripple in the soundscape changed the pulsating into something different. That's when I felt a single, multifaceted pulse overtake me, then shatter me into a thousand pieces.

My scattered pieces re-formed and took the shape of something that disgraced me as a human. I already knew I was in Hell; I was just trying to find my level in which to await all of eternity. The sky, if I can call it that, shone brighter. I stumbled in darkness, moving towards the light. The light became brighter and brighter. I lurched towards mountains of gold that seemed to shine forever.

I stood over a horizon and witnessed these mountains of gold that went on as far as the eye could see. I was in awe, not for the gold but for the expansiveness of it all.

I knew I was walking into the realm of Greed. I walked up to the first mountain and saw that it was constituted of gold coins, bars, jewelry, statues—anything and everything that sparkled as an item of worth that made men crazy.

I walked closer and closer. Another mountain of gold was ten yards away from it, and it comprised all the riches of a kingdom. Only ten yards away was another kingdom of gold, exactly as round and mischievous as the previous. Ten yards away was another... and then another. Each one was perfectly spaced from the next, and they stretched all the way to the horizon. I had never seen that wealth of riches nor even contemplated it.

Then the thrumming of the sound of Hell forced me to look elsewhere—not just at the golden piles themselves. I cast my eyes upward and finally caught a glimpse of what topped each mountain. I tried not to admit to myself what really was there, a mere thirty feet away. But when the something moved, I knew it bore a humanoid shape. It balanced precariously on the tip of the gold, trying not to disturb it, trying to keep the balance of all of the riches it owned by its own desire.

I took two steps backwards, and my eyes finally made out what it was: A human that was shriveled up, bones protruding from its skin and desperately hungry for something, something that could never be quenched. It stood there, staring out at the huge expanse of its own gold while also greedily staring at the other mountains of gold around it. I could see its face. I could see its pain, wanting to keep its riches but wanting the other pile of riches but also afraid to move.

Each piece of gold was like a stumbling block for this thing (I say "thing" because I could no longer accept them as human at this point). That's when I looked at the mountain next to it. I could see the same decrepit and desperate thing on the top of that mass of gold as well. I turned back to the immense pile in front of me and stared at the thing on top of it when it noticed me.

It saw me and I could see into its eyes. I could no longer consider them things, because I realized they were souls. I could see the pain and desire it had. It chilled me to the bone. My mind staggered as I saw this poor soul on top of his kingdom, afraid to move or disturb it for fear of losing it.

Then he moved. He didn't move much, just turning towards me, slowly like an enemy, perched on his mountaintop to protect it from me. His eyes widened in horror. His foot gently slid downward, an inch or two, and a jingling's worth of coins slipped down the mountaintop and rustled towards the bottom. I stepped backward because it was another sound that pierced my mind.

As I stepped back, I saw another soul. It seemed that they came out of nowhere, waiting at the bottom of each pile for a mistake. They looked exactly like those poor souls at the top of the mountains but they were hungrier. They didn't find themselves as rich as the poor souls at the top, so they waited at the bottom to pounce. Twenty to thirty gold coins finally fell off the mountain, and the desperate soul at the bottom grabbed them and ran. She ran precisely ten yards away, dumping them into a little pile.

The soul on top of the immense pile looked out in extreme anger, staring hard at the female soul, who grabbed his coins when he made another move. More coins jangled and shifted down the mountain but this time, another poor lost soul, on the other side, grabbed the bounty as it spilled to the bottom. He took what he could and made himself a little mound of seven to eight coins. He hovered over it, smacking his lips and rejoicing exactly ten yards away on the other side of the mountain.

This went on for more than I can say while I was watching them. I saw the have-nots steal a coin or more at a time, hoping to piss off the souls at the top so they would move and lose more of the riches on which they perched.

I walked backwards to take in more, and the expanse and sheer horror of understanding sunk into me.

Each mountain had three usurpers at the base, wanting to take gold from the soul on top. Each mountaintop had a gold worshipper that knew they were there but refused to give anyone anything because greed had overtaken him. Rulers of each pile took what they could from others until they virtually couldn't move without losing their riches to someone else. I had never seen it so clearly before.

After what felt like eons of watching this, one of them actually moved enough on the mountaintop, that he slipped along with the gold and riches that trickled down. He slid down the mountain to the bottom. As the gold bounced and clinked against itself, his yowls of anguish and pain filled the void, and one of the souls that waited desperately at the bottom climbed up the other side and made its way to the peak.

Then all the souls on all the mountains fell the same way, like rows of dominoes, ironically losing what they had in an attempt to keep it, giving those in wait a chance for their empires they had so greedily kept.

These dethroned mountaintop "kings" found themselves again with the paupers, desperately trying to start new mountains, always ten yards away. What was earlier a tinkling noise had become a roaring deluge of sound—the sound of gold falling and the screams of those losing and those taking. It was a sound of madness because it didn't stop. I couldn't believe what I was seeing but I did. It made too much sense and I began to feel faint.

The air crackled, and the world around me folded into itself while the dull throbbing of Hell pushed me to the next level. The Mountains of Greed washed away from my vision.

THE CHAMBERS OF GLUTTONY AND THE VALLEY OF LUST

I suddenly found myself in a huge room.

The stench of meat and rotten food enveloped me to the point of gagging on my own misery. My stomach twisted and turned as vomit left it, spewing out between my teeth. The vileness took hold as the rhythm of Hell infused my soul with a disgusting taste. (I can still taste it if I focus and try hard to remember.)

I retched and heaved until nothing was left inside me. Then I retched some more. I wiped tears from my eyes, and I looked up to see a monstrous beast.

This soul was humongous. This thing (again I say "thing" because I don't know what else to say), was a beast in Hell, over 3,000 pounds of disgusting humanity that took up the whole room I found myself in. It was surrounded by rotting meat, cheeses, fruits and every other edible, er, formerly edible object. It lay in its own waste, gorging on anything it could grab while stewing in its own juices. The stench was overwhelming due to bedsores and decay from its body.

I tried to wipe the spew from my mouth, but my heaving wouldn't stop. There was no stopping the gagging and vomit. I couldn't control it even when my so-called stomach had nothing left. The decay of burnt meat was overwhelming, and it was sickness personified. I tried to regain my composure as I looked at the lump of meat that someone had once called a body. I tried to step back but couldn't. This time, I was stuck in a room with the damned.

I should refer to this as a soul, but it was so buried deep down into that flesh that there was little to see anymore. I turned to the door and grasped the handle. It didn't turn when I twisted it, so I kicked it. It didn't give. I screamed at the door, desperately trying to get out. The sounds of eating and swallowing got louder. Each tear and chew of each decayed mouthful felt as if piece of me was bitten and chewed and swallowed down into a vat of acid, to be absorbed into something unholy.

The damn door wouldn't budge. I saw a number emblazoned at the top: 87,400,326. My mind rolled at that number. I fell to my knees and heard my insides yell, "WHAT THE FUCK!"

This soul just ate whatever it could grab. It was rotting as it breathed and chewed and didn't care as long as it got what it wanted. It just wanted food, mouth-watering food, and the gluttony turned the putrid food into heavenly deliciousness.

It was the slurping and chewing of a ravenous animal that couldn't get enough. I couldn't even see its arms past its heaving belly. It suddenly gagged, choked, and then retched all over itself, spewing vomit and half-eaten carcasses of animals all over itself. But it didn't stop eating. My curiosity got the best of me, so I walked around to see what it was doing and caught it eating the vomit stuck between its neck and chest, scooping it back into its mouth, swallowing and laughing while it did it.

After heaving some more, I ran back to the door and slammed against it, trying to get out. But the door still wouldn't budge. I ended up sliding down the doorframe and falling to my knees in desperation.

I was disgusted and overwhelmed but I managed to take a closer look at it. Then I saw that what I'd thought was a he was a she. It was a "lucky" glance (I didn't want to know but saw it all the same). My stomach was totally empty, but by this time, dry heaves suddenly became my specialty.

I turned around so I couldn't look any longer at that poor soul. All I could hear was the nomming, the slurping and the swallowing of unseen, disgusting food.

As I clutched my head, the scene before me began to dissolve like a fade in a movie.

I was left gasping for air and sanity, only to find neither. It was just a mess of humanity, caught in all its trappings and pitfalls. The thrumming sound shook me again and wouldn't let up. I slowly opened my eyes to see what was in front of me. I was no longer in the Chamber of Gluttony but somewhere else.

A convulsion began to emit from the lower tip of my spine and glided up my spinal column until I was a quivering mass of flesh encasing a skeleton I couldn't control.

Losing control of your body in Hell is a luxury you can't understand until you're there. Your mind, body and soul have been corrupted by the life and the society you lived in. When you finally lose control of what you're encased in, Hell ceases to be. All your synapses turn inwards, and the Hell you're in disappears.

You're swallowed whole and you're back into yourself as if you are alive. Just internally, mind you. Hell fades away for a moment, giving you a reprieve, or at least a breather. It's a gift that's hard to appreciate—that is, until you're there—before you're thrust in again; it's almost a torment. I wish this upon nobody, but as one of the damned, it's a sweet relief.

But again, it's just another devilish way to torment those in Hell. Slight spasms of the soul pull a person out of the horrifying consequences of eternal damnation, temporarily giving them the bliss of non-existence and total self-oblivion, only for that soul to be thrown back into the abyss. Cruelty knows no bounds in Hell, and I can attest to that.

I found myself on my knees, clutching myself as if I were a baby. I used every ounce of my reasoning to figure out what was going on: I've been in Hell for however long, but I was visited by God and tormented by the Devil for over a year. I have been on a quest for either salvation or damnation because I couldn't live my life any longer the way it was, without answers.

I found those, and my consequence was being here. For doing what I needed to make my life mean something, I was in Hell.

I stood up, with my eyes still closed. I slowly opened them. I could feel the emotion of this level and could feel a pang of what it was. I knew this was my level. I knew this was my personal sin!

The thrumming of the energy, the sound of the pulsations began to make sense. It's the same sound and pulsation I've felt my whole life. It's like vaguely knowing a nursery rhyme you heard as a kid and never quite making out what song it is, until you finally hear it clearly, and then you know that it's what has been driving you since the day you were born.

Every sin has a feel to it. Every man or woman is brought into the world with a propensity towards a certain sin being their major sin. We have secondary sins and we commit sins below our main one, but they're not like the true sin, which we feel comfortable with.

It's the sin we put on like clothes onto our naked soul. It's the sin we can easily make excuses for. And it's the sin—no matter what happens in life—we can still fall into very easily, especially at our worst but even at our best. We don the coat of sinfulness that we are born into, bred into, or fall into because it's a part of us, whether we hate it or not.

I'm telling you this because this is my sin. I felt it, felt comfortable with it, and knew I belonged here.

I slowly opened my eyes to the gyrations and the smell of sex.

Nothing could have prepared me for what I saw. I could taste it in the air. I could lose myself in every pleasure, desire and want I could ever imagine. I wasn't prepared for the sheer atrocity of an unrepentant orgy in Hell!

There were no demons, ringleaders or masters in this domain. It was an all-out frenzy of fucking, blowing, humping, licking and tasting of flesh that wanted to be desired and consumed in every pleasure imaginable.

Every soul wanted to lose itself in the act of love—to say nothing of the enslavement of love, spurred by yearning. It is the desire to possess another soul or body, to make it his or her own, even for a moment. It is the need to feel as if we are truly not alone in our own minds and that we can be connected during the act of sex. We still are very alone, even during the act of making love, but sometimes we are transformed and can finally feel close to something besides ourselves. Every now and then we need to be dominated, and sometimes we need to be submissive. Sometimes, we can play with sex as adults—just as kids used to play on the playground. Other times we can just show love and affection in the simple act of physical love and closeness we all desperately crave.

Once in a while, we need to feel dirty to feel alive. We need to cross taboos and do things we're told are wrong but which feel right when happening between two lovers. Lust falls into so many different spectrums of self-hatred and love of one another that it's one of the most confusing aspects of sin mankind has ever crossed.

The desperation of planting your seed and making sure your lineage is perpetuated is something men drive for, even if they don't want those specific things. The act of "sex to become pregnant" can drive some women to pregnancy with men they don't even know. Motherhood, fatherhood, and the need to give life, are programmed into all of us since birth.

The sin of lust can be connected to many things: Feeling loved, procreation, dominance or submissiveness, feelings of worth. You can feel abuse, torment and punishment while enjoying it. Love can be mixed up with sex—and the crazier the sex, the more you can feel that your partner loves you.

Lustful fantasies can bring a couple closer and maintain a bond, but without sex it can drive away, hurt, or even control a relationship. Sex can do so many amazing things and rip them all apart too. It's a fucking tightrope we walk daily.

How many wives or husbands have been cheated on? How many husbands and wives refuse to ask for what they really want, or need, sexually? How much of this timidity was from fear of judgment or of looking like a freak? How many souls have told their partners what they need sexually, only to be refused? How many people have strayed from their marriage to do what they're afraid to ask of their partners? How many people have committed adultery just for the simple feeling of neglect?

My mind was flooding with these thoughts as I watched the obscenity in front of me.

I don't think it is obscene to tell you the truth: My cock began developing a life of its own as I saw the massive wall of flesh that ranged farther than my eyes could see. Some people have seen an orgy in their life, even if only on the Internet; this made those look like child's play.

The bodies were raised 17 people high instead of the normal single layer of debauchery. Every body was on top of another body as they thrusted and took every inch and swallowed every juice from every orifice and genital you can imagine. Nothing was left to the imagination as every soul drank deep of their earthly desires, making them feel whole in the level of Hell we all call Lust.

Every breast was perfect, although some were man-made, as on Earth. All of them were flowing over abundantly to the point of extremism. Every female body was the exact size they desired on Earth, and every cock was as big as a horse's, as every man wishes.

If this seems too descriptive, it's done to explain the actuality of what I saw: Sexual pleasure to the point of obscenity. There was plenty more:

Every woman was taking multiple cocks and swallowing every impossible inch. There was no gag reflex unless the female soul wanted it. No man ejaculated prematurely unless the woman was begging for him to come. And no body turned anything down. They were lost in the sin.

The orgy of Hell makes the debauchery of Earth feel like a tepid warm-up exercise. Body heaped onto body as if they were almost weightless.

As for the amount of cum, it was everywhere and each cock seemed to pump a gallon of it wherever it was sprayed. It was swallowed, buried and squirted out of every hole that was offered. It was spread on oversized tits and asses, to be licked off by hungry nymphomaniac women desperately needing to taste the cum of men.

The sweaty pleasure of anxious, desperate sex was almost too much to bear. I wanted to jump in. I wanted to lose myself in the sins of the flesh and make my fantasies come true, because here it was, right in my reality. Everything I wanted and desired was in my grasp.

But I knew I was in Hell. I knew I was merely an observer. God knew my sins, and he wasn't testing me. He was telling me what I could look forward to. He might have even been telling me this is how he sees me.

My cock was almost in my hand, but it wasn't, even though I'd never been so hard in my life. I knew Dante Alighieri didn't jerk off in Hell, but perhaps Hell had changed since he visited.

It makes me feel alive while lost in the sin of lust. I am and always will be totally and unequivocally disoriented by the sins of the flesh.

I continued watching the voluntary damned go at it like dogs in heat. Just from my vantage point, I could see double vaginal, double anal, foursomes, threesomes, bukkake, gangbangs, swapping, switching, masturbators and voyeurs all in the same sex act, at the same time. Every soul was desperate to be used and to be abused by everyone while using and abusing others in the same thrust or breath.

Then I saw it. I didn't understand at first, but after I saw it multiple times and after inspecting closely, I knew I was seeing female-male gender switches. One minute a man was a woman, and the next a woman was a man. It was as if everyone could switch to feel the other perspective, and nobody really noticed it because everyone was deep into the act.

After a while, I walked around this pile of prurient souls, hoping to find the end. I did, but then I noticed more piles of souls beyond, also screwing each other into oblivion. They were all just going through the act—nothing more. Orgasms would squirt and shiver all over everyone, but their desperate need to want and to be wanted achieved nothing. There was no afterglow. There was no stopping or laughing or appreciation of the closeness shared. They were totally desperate to stay in the act. Piles of women, for instance, ate each other out and kissed, but after each orgasm, they shifted to someone else to try to feel loved.

I also saw the man pile. Didn't want to, but I did. They were fucking and sucking, taking load after load but never feeling quenched or satiated. They just moved to another body after each orgasm.

I could see other piles in the distance and some were filled with more fetish-dominated souls. Others were just like the one in front of me. I stopped looking at the others and just turned around to examine the pile closest to me.

No orgasm that I saw let a soul feel complete. In the desperation of wanting to feel connected, it made the soul even more alone. Every orgasm, kiss and grope gave way to more needing.

I walked closer to the pile of bodies and began to look them in the face as they fucked themselves in the Devil's bedroom.

I saw exasperation in their faces. I saw loneliness and tears of unfulfilled feelings. The act of what should have been love was an act of sorrow and loss. I could see it in their eyes, always trying to recapture a feeling but mistaking it for the act itself.

I could see those whose lives were in shambles; the manipulative conquest of someone needing to be loved was used to make their egos feel better about themselves.

My heart dropped as I saw it for what it truly was. I saw the self-hatred and how the act of sex became the act of dominance resulting from this self-hatred. They had all lost the meaning of love and had replaced it with the act of sex. They couldn't feel the beauty of it; they had lost sight of that.

This was the majority of what I saw, but the piles were filled with others. Lust is the craziest of all sins, because it falls into so many different patterns and desires that it began to make my head throb.

That's another reason lust is an easy sin to commit: We all feel alone, even when married, engaged or dating. We are locked into our own minds. We may try to show a partner who we are and what we need, but we truly can't say it all. There is no way we can, due to our own circumstances. We can argue and fight over it and give ultimatums. We can tell our loved ones who we are and what we need, but it rarely works without extreme devotion and love.

This doesn't mean your sexual requests fall on deaf ears; they just fall on ears that are not yours. That is why, when true closeness during sex is achieved, it can make such headway towards keeping love and closeness between two people. Sex, as long as it is done with love and not hatred for one's self or hatred towards the other, can be the most awe-inspiring thing God has ever created.

That's why it can take us over. Sex, whether loving or twisted, can make us blind to the reality around us and put us in the here and now. We give ourselves over to the act. It gives lovers those minutes, seconds and even hours to forget the outside world. It's probably why God gave us only seconds during the actual orgasm.

The complete loss of reality and the complete closeness of another individual—even for just a couple of seconds—is to remind us of what Heaven can be like, to remind us of how it feels to be accepted, respected and loved.

I walked past the bodies and around them. The sounds began grating on my nerves. I tried to look around, but aside from the desperate bodies, all I could see was darkness.

I began to run when I saw what I thought was an opening. I ran for it and then stumbled into it. I fell down and began to roll down a steep incline. I was falling down the side of a mountain in the utter darkness and out of the Valley of Lust.

THE MAZE OF VANITY

I didn't know where I found myself, because I was lost.

I've been lost physically, and I've been lost emotionally, and I certainly have been lost spiritually. I wouldn't be on this ride if I hadn't.

But the sort of lost I found there meant everything was lost.

No hope, no life. Hope and life are all we have, and they were taken away from me. I lost everything important to me, and I found myself in a place where I knew I belonged, and it was different.

You figure Hell is place that you're exiled and banished to. But it's a place that welcomes you with open arms. It takes you for who you are. It takes you and lets you sink into the mire of what it is you actually want.

I started to notice a pattern in Hell that began to make me sick. I saw it on the souls' faces as it began to become apparent in everyone who was here long enough. All souls that turned away from God got exactly what they wanted. Their sins were magnified a hundredfold, and at first they're grateful for an endless supply of what they think they want. But having it all really doesn't give them what they want. Lots of sex, eating, or wealth just makes a soul realize that more is out there.

I saw sins for what they truly are: virtues that can lead to vices. Then, of course, vices can lead to worse vices. I saw the actual makeup of virtue and the sins that overloaded us as human beings. We let sin step in and take control of us, even when we think we are doing virtue. I didn't have much time to ponder this aspect, but it was enough to show me I was in store for more of this formula.

I felt the internal rumble that shook me while electricity and blackness enveloped me. I screamed a scream of Hellish proportions that still sickens me to this day.

Calmness finally overtook me, and I found myself standing in front of a hall of mirrors. I peered in and could see it was a maze of mirrors stretching before me. I walked in.

I stopped at the gateway and stared for a moment at the reflections surrounding me. I began to notice what seemed like a visual hiccup. I could see through the mirrors to the souls on the other side of them. But they were backwards, as if the mirror was showing me what the people see from their side.

I took a deep breath and walked through the gateway. When a mirror shattered next to me, it felt as if my soul shattered too. A millisecond later, the shards of my mind did splinter into a million jagged pieces then solidified, forming back into myself. At the same time, the mirror's fractures rippled and became whole again.

I fell to my knees. I knew that every crack in my mind had repaired itself just so it could break me into a million pieces again.

My psyche shattered again, and I could feel each and every distinct piece of my personality break off. I could see, to my horror, that what I thought was me was actually a diverse makeup of ideas, thoughts and feelings that was too numerous to even comprehend. All the mirrors broke around me, and I could see aspects of myself in every splinter and shard. They began to meld back into a whole and, simultaneously, so did my mind.

My consciousness was on the verge of a meltdown. I gasped as rotten air inflated my lungs. I tried to stand back up, only to stumble. I raised myself to a full, upright position while my eyes darted around, expecting me to break again. Mirrors extended as far as the eye could see, so I walked deeper into the maze.

I didn't make it far. Disillusionment and disfigured beauty rolled over me like a freight train. I fell to my knees again, clutching my chest, desperately trying to hold myself together. I didn't want to shatter again. What happened if my pieces couldn't re-form?

The reality of this place sank in. Terror filled the void in my heart with the fear of Hell that could never be squelched.

I stood again and walked forward in the maze, when I began to hear them. I could hear the soft voices all around me. I could hear how beautiful, how enchanting they all were, speaking to themselves.

I knew where I was—the level of Vanity. I was in the level where people loved themselves more than anything else in the world. It was an ego trip heavily connected to appearances, because if you believe you're beautiful, you have self-worth in your own mind.

The straight path split, and I took a right. I followed my gut because not only was I in a maze of mirrors, I was in a maze of mirrors in Hell itself. I expected up to be down, right to be left, and that walking forwards would lead me backwards. Continuing down my chosen path a while longer, I stopped.

It was at an edge, an actual corner of the maze, and I didn't see anyone outside of the mirrors. I thought I had been seeing through the mirrors to people on the other side, but they were actually *in* the mirrors. If I looked at a mirror from the front and then looked at the back, the image was reversed on either side. I stood there for a moment and listened to a poor woman who was trapped in the mirror before me.

I could hear her talk about her beauty. She talked to herself about how wonderful she was, because she looked so attractive. Everyone bowed down to her, and she could do anything she wanted—all because of her stunning vivaciousness. I felt sick upon realizing she was worshipping herself.

I wasn't looking at her at the time. I was looking downwards, paying attention to her words as they flowed in and out of my consciousness. I heard enough and looked up at the woman in the mirror.

The mirror was wavering and shimmering as if trying to break but unable. The woman's form breathed in and out, changing from grotesque to beautiful. The changes occurred in the space of a second. I watched the play and listened to the act. I needed to see what she actually was. I could hear what she believed she was, but I saw something confusing staring back at me from the mirror.

We caught gazes, and she stopped. She laughed to herself.

"I know you love what you see," she said.

I tried to shift my eyes away, but I was locked in her gaze.

I said, "I see what you are."

She laughed and said, "I know. That's why I know you love me."

I stepped back, still looking into her eyes, and felt nauseous. I could see her for what she truly was. I couldn't see it before, but I could finally see the horrors of what she had lost. Her face and body featured scabs and open, oozing sores. Every feature on her face contorted into something more hideous every second I looked. I tried to take my eyes off her, because I couldn't understand what she was putting herself through.

I'm a decent-looking guy. Nothing Adonis would write home about, but I don't consider myself ugly. But I have never preened over myself for hours in front of a mirror. And I've never taken more than 20 seconds to pick out clothes. I never thought my looks made me feel important. Or, at least that's what I think. I feel I'm good-looking because of who I am. My personality trumps anything my physical body offers. I've been fat, overweight, normal, svelte, and buff, but I have never based my self-worth on my looks.

I began realizing things about myself I never knew: When it came down to it, my outward shell barely had an impact on who I am. Of course, you want to look perfect or at least to look better, but it has never stopped me from doing anything in my life.

I looked at the soul in the mirror, and she wasn't looking at me anymore. She was staring at herself in her mirrored trap. Only it wasn't a trap for her. It was exactly what she wanted—to be with the most important person in the world: herself.

I walked down the corridor to the corner and turned with it. I made a series of lefts and rights, trying to get to the middle. Mirrors of self-important people surrounded me as I heard what they were saying to themselves:

"I am the best, and nobody can do the things I do."

"I make myself look good, because it's what's important to me."

"I'm just wonderful."

"I'm so beautiful."

"I'm smarter than everyone I know."

I had to stop at this point. I was lost, confused and aghast at what I had been hearing. What I told you was a drop in the bucket, because I could hear many, many voices at the same time. None of them could hear anyone else, though—not even from the adjacent mirrors.

Then something dawned on me about the Vain who were trapped in these mirrors. They were just as lost as I was. The difference was, they were lost in their own minds, and I was lost in this maze.

I picked someone to listen to, and I could hear their thoughts scurrying around in a maze of their beliefs, refusing to find a way out. Each soul was inside its own maze, inside this maze of mirrors. I shivered.

I stopped and tried to gain my bearings, but it seemed impossible. I could hear millions of people lost in their own minds, not crying or wanting any interaction besides their own.

I began to lose it because I didn't have a clue where I was, lost in the maze of reflections of the damned. I clenched my fists and my jaw, almost shattering my teeth. I was hoping my teeth cracking would wake me out of this Hell.

Then I closed my eyes. I prayed to God at this time and found myself slowly coming to peace. My eyes were closed and it felt as if I wasn't lost, that I had never been lost at all.

The voices were still talking to themselves. I kept my eyes closed and looked around in the darkness of myself. I slowly turned my body around in a circle as I stood there.

I saw a hint of light behind my eyelids. I spun around again and continued until I saw the light, still faint.

I stopped, focusing on the tiny white light. I opened my eyes and was flooded with only mirrors, lost souls, and the loving torment of which they convinced themselves.

I began to panic but didn't move. I slowly closed my eyes again. Darkness rolled across me. I could see the white light again. I opened my eyes to the cacophony of narcissistic Hell then closed them again as fast as I could.

My mind raced for my escape. I was lost, surrounded by mirrors of the damned, in the middle of a fucking maze. At least I thought it was the middle.

But when I closed my eyes, I knew where to go. I felt it and wasn't ashamed or fearful of it. I knew what I had to do.

I squeezed my eyes tighter and I took one step towards the light. Nothing happened, so I took another step.

Nothing happened. So I took two steps, then three and four. I stopped and listened to the rabble of the self-loving.

"I'm the best and no one can do this but me."

"People should love me because I'm a model and have been in four advertisements."

"People will never like me because they're jealous of me."

I refused to open my eyes. I didn't know what I was doing, so I took another five steps.

I stopped again. The light was a bit closer but still seemed an eternity away. I knew I should've hit a mirror 15 steps ago, but I hadn't.

I opened my eyes and saw the maze twist and turn away from me 13 paces ago, as if I went backwards and forwards at the same time. I had to test it out more, because it already seemed like it worked. Even though I was lost again in my visual interpretation.

I closed my eyes. The white light in the darkness of my vision flared up in front of me as I stepped forward. I took another slow step and then another. I almost began to chuckle but thought against it with my next step.

I walked towards that small light I could see with my eyes closed, actually gaining momentum in each stride. It was as if it was 100 yards away, and each step was a yard and a half. But it wasn't.

I walked with my eyes closed for so long I didn't have a sense for where I was any more. Following the white light became excruciating, so I had to stop. I took a breath and opened my eyes, very slowly.

Mirrors on all sides surrounded me. The trapped souls were even viler than they'd been at the beginning of the maze, and I could hear:

"I'm the most famous person on the planet."

"People worship me."

"I'm more beautiful than god."

"Everyone will bow down because I am everything to everyone."

"I am my own god."

I choked on my own bile. I closed my eyes again, and the light was as it was, so I took a couple of steps again.

Nothing hit me, nothing stopped me. I could still hear what they said, though. I began walking towards the light again. I realized it was an open space as long as I didn't look or use my eyes.

I fucking ran for it. I didn't care if I hit anything. I didn't care if I hurt myself. I had to escape, lest I be stuck here. I fretted about the thought of falling into a mirror and loving myself into damnation.

My stride hit a peak, and the light got closer and closer until I slammed into a wall. I hit it hard and was knocked to the floor, causing my jaw agonizing pain. I thought I had knocked my teeth loose, so I tried to wiggle my teeth with my tongue. They didn't move.

I almost laughed my ass off at this point; Here I am, worried about knocking my teeth loose in Hell when a demon would be more than happy to yank them with pliers, one by one, only to shove them back in so as to repeat the process.

I didn't know where I was, but I knew I'd hit something that stopped me, so I opened my eyes to see the stone wall of a tunnel. I had actually hit something physically normal. I turned backwards to see the route I had taken. There was the maze, sitting in all of its Hellish glory. I could hear the chatter and the praises but more in a "distant stadium rabble" way than the one-on-one conversations I had heard inside.

I turned back towards the entrance of the tunnel and I expected to see a light or something that had guided me from the maze but there wasn't anything.

Trying to think how things work in Hell, I closed my eyes and looked around, everywhere.

I saw a new light that wasn't there before. This time it was a red speckle. It was shining from the direction I had come, and I stared at it for a reasonable amount of time, thinking.

I made up my mind, opened my eyes and turned back towards the tunnel's entrance. I walked up to the gateway, to the cold and barren stone.

I didn't know what was on the other side of that tunnel but I either had to find my place in Hell, or find my way through Hell. I also didn't know if I was dying or if I was already dead. My mind recounted my visitation by God so maybe this is something He wanted to show me, something I needed to know.

All I knew was I had to press onward. I began to walk into it. My soul shifted and I felt something I had known before but had never wanted to acknowledge. I felt another of my major sins crawling up my vertebrae, just as it had when nestling in my head a thousand times before. I took a deep breath, possibly the deepest breath ever taken in Hell. I stepped over the threshold and out of the Maze of Vanity.

THE CAVERN OF SLOTH

I walked past the gateway into what I already knew. I could feel it in my bones, because it gave me a metallic taste in my mouth as I took my first couple steps. My ears began to ring, and my mouth became dry. I took a couple more steps, and the ringing spread to my head. The metallic taste turned to cinnamon, which tasted good. My bones began to lighten, and I felt better as each step took me deeper. My mouth began to produce saliva again, and I felt normal again.

I walked and trotted into the tunnel and felt good, felt right. It was unlike anything I had ever felt before, even when I had been alive on earth. I felt as if I belonged and as if I was going where I should. I just marched along to a beat of a drum I'd never heard before.

But as I walked towards my destination, my mind began nagging at me. It somehow felt "roomy" in my head. Something wasn't right but I still kept going.

Over the course of 20 steps, I began to notice something. I couldn't put my finger on it, but I could feel it. My thoughts raced at a million miles per hour, but my body acted as if it was going at normal speed. Then my body wasn't even managing normal speed. I was barely moving.

My steps were in slow motion while my mind was fast as ever. Ideas and thoughts where careening towards each other and smashing into the realm of time and space I call my mind. It has never raced so supersonically relative to my body.

I tried to think slower, comparing it to my body. I tripped and then slowly fell forward, but my mind produced hours', maybe even days' worth of thoughts in the time it took me to fall.

Madness tugged at me during my slow-motion fall. I was going insane due to the gap between my body's reaction and my mind's rapidity of thought.

As I hit the floor, I felt a rash of spikes, glass and jagged edges penetrate my flesh, ever-so-slowly.

My mouth gradually produced a slow-motion scream of agony. The feeling of a wound gradually worsening is infinitely more painful than quick nick. A normal injury is fast and sudden, and the mind doesn't have a chance of keeping up with the pain as it happens. This was the exact opposite—realizing every millisecond of the pain and infliction your body takes, knowing you are unable to stop it, while the injury grows worse.

The glass and metal slid increasingly deeper into my flesh, and I was at the mercy of my own racing mind. My eyes were the only part of my body that operated at normal speed. I saw the whole floor was embedded with glass, spikes, and jagged pieces of rusty metal. My hands slowly raised themselves, trying to break my fall, and I could see that they were headed straight for pain and injury.

I felt glass slowly dig into my flesh, each millimeter digging deeper and deeper over what seemed like hours, days. Each new piece of metal and glass touched my skin for what felt like an eternity before slowly puncturing my skin. Then another one, half an inch away from the previous, would touch me. As the first one sunk in, the pressure of the next split the skin.

My hands and forearms began to hit, and the slow, deliberate shredding of my flesh continued. The sharpness pierced my torso. I felt the spikes and glass scrape against my bones. My consciousness couldn't handle it any more. I tried to black out but couldn't.

But the days/weeks/years of suffering eventually yielded a new approach: A willing acceptance of the slow-motion damage occurring to my body. During the eons I had to think about it, the more I realized just to accept the pain and blood as a fact of my reality.

At some point, the glass and metal couldn't go any farther into my body. My flesh had shredded and my veins had split, causing blood to flow in slow motion. My face had hit into jagged and serrated spikes that mauled my cheekbone, jaw but, thankfully, not my throat. My body had given up, and I had fallen flat onto the floor of the cave. I finally slammed into place.

That's when time changed; my body picked up a little speed but still was lagging behind my mind. I screamed and tried to wiggle out, but my arms and legs were stuck. In fact, I didn't even notice this about my appendages at the time, as I was more concerned with my impaled face. In any case, I had been slammed onto a surface made to incapacitate a man, much like a flytrap for a fly. I was stuck, wanting to pull free but unable.

I could feel my blood seep out of me with each and every tug. I flailed and flopped but couldn't get out. I was stuck like a fish on a hook. It actually felt like a thousand hooks and probably was. My racing mind tried to make sense of what I was going through. That's when it happened.

I stopped moving so the blood would slow its spillage. I began to lie perfectly still, accepting my fate. I let my body relax. I let everything slide deep into my body. And then I felt it:

The pain began numbing itself, and the sharp spikes and tidbits of glass started feeling as if they weren't there anymore. The more I gave up, the less I moved, the more the pain went away. My muscles relaxed, and my damaged bones felt as if it had never happened. Even the bleeding stopped if I stayed still.

I lost every bit of drive. It was as if trying hurt. Moving and living was a pain. I was finally in a place where I could give it all up.

I lay there, breathing. I was ready to accept this as my final resting place. Any movement brought me agony, and all stillness brought me relief. I laid there for what seemed like decades. I gave my mind a pass to stop thinking. I'd never been able to stop thinking, during prayer, stillness, or even bedtime. I'd never been able to turn off my imagination. But here, finally, I could.

I did, though, think about what I had done and what I had hoped to do. I realized that what I was doing—standing still, not bettering my place in the universe—went against all my beliefs. So I latched onto a thought that was zooming around my head, believing in me. I slowed it down to grab it, as it was a hard thought to grab; grasping it brought pain and disappointment. Grasping this thought didn't necessarily mean I was going to reach the Promised Land. It didn't mean my hard work would actually become something.

Millions of people work their asses off, only to fail. Hard work and dedication don't always pay off, but if you never try, then you will always hate yourself. So you fail, grab the horse and jump back on. You might fall back off and get stomped on, and you might never succeed. If everyone got what they wanted, nobody would be working; everyone would be famous and rich.

This thought stung me like a hive of yellow jackets. That's when I became mad. Mutilating-my-flesh mad. I pushed myself up, ripping my flesh and what felt like part of my soul. I could feel muscle and sinew pull out of me. Every wound screamed in unrelenting pain. My face was ripped apart from the serrated metal and glass, but it was a freedom I had never felt before. Blood poured out like a waterfall, but I kept going.

My hands grabbed on to the side of the cave wall, and I pulled myself up. I was off the floor of Hell. My exhausted body was desperate to fall back down, but my freedom and desire outweighed any secondary thoughts of respite.

I looked for a place to set my foot down after I had ripped it free. That's when the tunnel began to melt. It wasn't the rock structure of the tunnel that melted but merely the jagged edges and metallic spikes. My left foot was the last to break free, but it didn't pull itself off; the spikes dissolved inside it.

I lifted my hands to my face, expecting a mutilated mess. I felt an urgency to fit the skin back over my face, but it wasn't necessary. My fingers touched my face and found it whole again.

Faded, out-of-focus images took shape. The cavern was as deep as I thought it was. I could see the tunnel and the pit I'd walked into. But I also began to see other people, stuck to the floor of Hell as I had been. I breathed a sigh of pain and cried.

I took a step, and the nearby spikes and glass shimmied away from my foot. It was tough, but I forced myself to take another step. The sharpness crawled away from me again but stayed as close to my flesh as it could without cutting me. I took another and another until I was in full stride. I began to smile, that is until I looked at all who had come before me.

I listened and heard the sighs of people content, not moving. I could tell they heard me but acknowledgment of me would bring pain, and pain would bring sorrow, and sorrow would bring more pain. I don't know why I had been able to get out of that trap. Its allure is powerful. Its trappings are way too easy.

The tunnel kept going down, and the sections became more elaborate. The tunnel became a cavern, and the cavern was filled with cubicles. I passed men and women sitting on barbed-wire chairs in front of blank computer screens. The cubicles gave way to living rooms, with people—impaled on spikes and glass fixed to cement couches—sitting before golden television sets. They were staring but not moving, no matter what was on the glowing screens. Glowing screens faded into beds and even the inside of cars, as people sat or lay there, afraid to do anything. They were afraid to live and try and fail, because failure is always an option. Every soul I saw stayed where it was. They were all impaled on their own jagged feelings of failure, and temptations to waste time and energy kept them stuck in the lower confines of Hell.

I was passing by a seat. I stopped. I looked at the man sitting there and could tell he could see me. His flesh was stabbed onto the sharpness of Hell. I saw his eyes turn to me, without his body moving. He looked, then shifted his eyes away. I took a step or two towards him. The blades flowed away like water.

"What you are you still doing here?" I asked. "You can see me and you can feel me walk past you. You don't have to stay here anymore. You are free if you want to go."

He closed his eyes and a small whimper eked out of his throat. He took another couple of seconds and croaked, "It has been an eternity now, so I have to answer you so that you will leave me alone. Why would you torment a man like me for thousands of years by asking me a question and standing there, for untold eons?"

My mind realized the Hell he was in. I was stuck in that Hell for what seemed like centuries when it was likely only a matter of seconds. My heart bled for him.

"I am so sorry for tormenting you for so long."

I turned around and walked away as quickly as I could. I thought about the man. If he'd experienced 10,000 years in the seconds I'd told him of his potential freedom, and if he had 10,000 years to refuse to get up, then he was truly lost.

Before leaving his earshot, I called back, "You can get up and get out of here. It's ultimately more painful to remain, because the pain of doing nothing is even worse than doing something."

The cavern turned towards a tunnel. I headed towards it while the sharpness ran from my feet. I began to wonder what it was I was truly in. As my steps became faster, I closed my eyes for a second, only to see the small hint of white light in front of me. I turned my head around and looked with closed eyes, only to see a speck of red, far behind me.

I opened my eyes and walked out of the Cavern of Sloth. The air hit me, but unlike the gusts of winds to which I was accustomed, the air wasn't fresh. It wasn't invigorating, and I didn't feel safe.

THE AUDITORIUM OF THE ENVIOUS

I walked out of the mouth of the cavern, breathing a stink that almost dropped me to my knees; I couldn't inhale without grimacing.

I saw a doorway on top of a cliff, and I suddenly found myself standing before it. The door was solid rock and about ten feet high with symbols engraved around the frame. I approached, and the doorway expanded to twenty feet high and seven feet wide. Then the door opened.

A "bright darkness" shone from it. My eyes tried to adjust, and I lost all my thoughts at this point. I walked up to the doorway and passed through and was several steps into the landscape when it hit me.

Envy. It crept up on me while trying to showcase itself to my soul. But it was not a sin that ever truly registered in my life.

The famous had tried their best on me by showing me their riches. They had fame and wealth to the point of opulence but it didn't work. I was more than happy for them, that they had more than I could possibly dream of. Would it be nice? Probably. Who doesn't want be rich or famous? But it's certainly nothing to kill over, or ruin your life. So I understood envy somewhat. But I didn't let it control me, even when it has reared its ugly head to me.

Music and lights surrounded me. I didn't know if I was coming or going. I tried to stand there, to make sense of it all, but I couldn't.

I found myself in a horde of people, ramping up and discharging all of the energy they had. I was lost in a sea of want and neglect that I couldn't comprehend.

I was stuck in this crowd, unsure of exactly where I was. I held my breath and pushed forward. The throngs of people were intense. The inhabitants who surrounded me were lost in something I couldn't understand, even when I had figured it out. I was still confused.

I knew this was meant to show envy, but it was harder for me to see how this reflected the sin and how it affected my life. I saw a gargantuan stage and three pedestals for four lucky souls, the ones they elevated. I saw everyone else kneeling, and I felt them praying.

They were praying to something I couldn't comprehend. They were praying to something even they didn't understand; they only knew they wanted and desired it. They wanted to understand how the few above them had things that should have been theirs.

I tried to work my way through everyone, but it seemed impossible. It was like trying to make your way to the front of a concert. Souls refused to move. Everyone was angry because of what they didn't have or who they weren't.

The music suddenly changed, and the elevated souls drifted down from their pedestals and from the stage. The masses beneath trembled. Then they mutated, with horns erupting from their heads and new mouths ripping apart their jawbones, turning them into gaping maws of vicious teeth.

They began jumping upward, trying to eat those they desired. I watched as a woman's leg was torn off and swallowed whole by another woman. Arms were ripped off then used as clubs to beat the torsos of those they coveted.

Blood and organs slipped out of open wounds on the formerly elevated bodies. The envious lower souls continued to eat and dismember those of whom they were jealous.

The remains were eventually gone, and the masses stood up, staring at the ceiling. Lights began to blaze, and music began to thunder, and they all started fighting amongst each other for the honor of being envied.

The souls were every bit as vicious during this stage. Terrified, I pushed my way out of the crowd, heading for a corner I saw out of the side of my eye. I was so deep in the masses of envy that I could only find that one escape route. But it wasn't an escape; it was a defensive position. I fought my way towards it.

I was almost there when a seven-foot creature jumped into my way, preparing to tear me apart. I saw it for a mere second, turning my head quickly so I wouldn't look at it. Seeing that I didn't care about him, it jumped on someone next to me and buried its claws into that soul's stomach, which ripped apart like an exploding water balloon.

I shielded my eyes away from the explosive gore around me. As the fighting became nasty, I made my way into the corner of this place. I hunkered down, putting my back to the wall.

I sat for what seemed like hours while the fighting sounded increasingly intense. Finally, my curiosity got the best of me, so I stood up to see what was going on.

It was a madhouse. Bodies were everywhere. Everybody's visage was altered to some extreme. I stared at the desperation in the souls left alive, and I began to notice some of them were more demonic then others.

I saw a man and a woman fighting each other. She was covered in scales. Her mouth was immense and had protruding teeth. The man just had small horns and claws; he was almost normal in appearance.

150

Compared to her, he was nothing. She picked him up and stuck his head into her mouth. It was clear what I was seeing. Those who let envy overcome every aspect of who they are, were the most transformed. Those who had allowed envy to destroy their lives but not the lives of others, were more human looking.

She clamped down and bit his head off. His neck stump spewed blood, spurting to the beat of the music. She found another victim near her and bit half his torso off.

She threw them onto the pile of bodies. The bodies amassed until only five of the envious were left standing.

I tried to think of what the sin of envy can do, and I realized many people are murdered over envy—envy of their possessions, spouses or even fame.

I watched as the five survivors stood over the fallen. They were the most satanic, deformed atrocities I have ever seen. They were the worst of the worst, and they all looked at each other, because they knew: There could only be four of them. I saw three pedestals and only one stage. They all began to hyperventilate, and right when I thought they were going to pass out, they charged at each other like runaway freight trains. Claws and teeth ripped and shredded each other until one of the five was ripped apart. The four screamed with Hellish delight.

The chamber—an arena, really—began to hum of its own accord. The dead began to shift and murmur. Wounds healed and limbs reattached in a grotesque dance of the macabre. The dead were alive again, and their monstrous forms were no more.

The music started, and the four winners floated up to the envious positions of the stage and pedestals. Their demonic features faded, beauty and wonder emanating in their place. I noticed that the head-biting woman had taken the main stage. Lights shone on her, and she glittered and dazzled.

I hid in that corner of stone while thinking; I had to understand what was going on. As I watched the last of the souls get comfortable on their pedestals, I wondered how long they stayed being envied by the masses?

I thought about my own responses to envy and what I actually envied. I knew what I should do. Maybe, just maybe I could get out of there.

The souls below shuffled and pushed roughly around each other, not caring about anything except for those who were elevated to something beyond them.

The pedestals moved under the feet of the envied. The light shone onto them like rock stars, and the souls beneath,—dead until a few moments ago—now prayed at their feet. They also begged and wanted to do anything to be elevated.

I turned and looked for a way out, and I believe I saw it. I prayed it was the exit. I stepped over the huddled masses, who never realized they were as good, or even better, than the people they put on the pedestals.

As I passed one of the pedestals, I finally looked at an elevated soul up close. I took a look to see what was so enviable about him, and I could immediately feel it in my bones. This man was better than me. He had a bigger house, better kids, and his wife was gorgeous. What's more, he does exactly what he wants as a job. It was cake, and he made a fortune, giving him vacations, mistresses, and the American Dream. I walked past him towards the next soul on a pedestal.

Her pedestal was even higher than the man's. As I neared, I could feel a psychic backlash from her slam into me. The envy was even worse. Her life consisted of perfect kids, a perfect life, and she always gave her husband more than he asked for. She was there for every kid's party, doing whatever she wanted while also being the head of a household. It was perfect in every way. She was a size one, her shoes were a size two and they were Gucci. Everything about her screamed that she had made it. No one could come close to her libido, her closeness with her family, her love for her husband, or the chores she did while working as a full-time actress.

At least, that is what everyone saw and believed. So envy gnawed at the insides of everyone around her.

I turned towards the exit. The envious didn't want to leave, so the exit from this Hell was plainly marked. I continued towards it and wasn't looking back when I heard the blast.

It was a huge rippling that crossed everyone around me. I had to turn to see it (I was lucky not to have turned into a pillar of salt).

I saw the envied ripped apart again by the mutated envious. The demonic war to be among the envied was starting over.

I stumbled and fell and began to crawl towards the exit. It was another stone doorway. Before I crawled through, I closed my eyes. I saw the faint white light in front of me. I turned behind me and saw the faint red light at the other end. This had become my cue, so I lurched through the doorway.

I thanked God.

My soul dropped into myself. There was nowhere else to go but into myself. That's when I realized I was on the last level of Hell. At least, that's what I hoped.

I turned and walked away from the Auditorium of the Envious, down the next tunnel into another Hell.

THE MISUNDERSTANDING AND THE UNDERSTANDING OF HELL

I had no clue what to expect. I wanted to stop walking, but my legs wouldn't let me. I tried figuring what sins were left, but most thoughts eluded me. I was confused; your mind and memories flash through you when you're in Hell.

"I saw Lust, right? I saw that?"

I felt my cock go hard. I knew I'd visited the level of lust because my body reacted to it.

"I visited Envy."

My cock suddenly shriveled up, trying to hide inside of me. I figured I must have been there, as my body reacted to the thought of it too. But I was still disoriented. Couldn't think properly. I tried to stop and think, but my legs kept walking.

"Pride? Have I seen Pride?"

My thoughts began to anger me because they weren't giving me answers. What I had was a hunch, but that wasn't reliable.

I took another step. A feeling of dread and hatred washed over me. Flames began to erupt all around me, and I tried to jump back. But my legs kept pushing onwards. Molten rock and sounds of anger permeated the strait I traveled as it opened to something else. Something I wasn't prepared for. My thoughts of pride swiftly fell to my side as an unknown hatred overcame me.

Each step closer shook me. Tumultuous thoughts raced around my head as if a swarm of bees encircled me. Thoughts focused on past deeds, horrifying scenarios that were done to me and to those I cared about. Some were by accident and others were on purpose.

The fire overcame me and wrapped around me, engulfing me in an ever-loving hatred for those who'd harmed me.

My flesh caught fire. And I felt a fire blaze inside me because that's all it could do: Eat me from the inside and bring out anger and hate into a boiling state that left only one thing inside of me.

Rage. Rage towards those who hurt me or had tried. I had never felt it so exquisitely in my life. Anger and wrath were all summed up in a fiery furnace that was once my soul.

My legs finally stopped and I just stood there, a dripping mess of abhorrence, annihilation, and vengeance that began to crawl everywhere around me.

That's when I saw them.

Other souls were caught up in this hatred and self-pity that were at the bottom of this pit. Every soul's wrath burned into eternity. The soul closest to me was a maelstrom of liquid fire. I watched his soul undulate as the inferno grew inside him while spreading to burn everyone around him. It was as if a volcano erupted behind his pupils and towards my own.

As his wrath burned towards me, mine reacted, spewing back towards him. The flames engulfed each other and took parts of us away. Others around us started doing the same to us. That made the anger inside of all of us bubble even more.

My personal fire scorched and ate into the souls around me, and their feelings of wrath needed to consume me. In turn, the fire of my soul began to reach farther into the pit, reaching into others who hadn't harmed me yet; their fire was just there. I needed to consume and so did they.

My spirit was no longer my own. The flames of anguish burned and wanted revenge on all who were there, ready to consume me in a blaze of their own hatred.

Even though they burned those around them, the burning didn't register as an attack, so when they were attacked in turn, they felt transgressed and were indignant. The conflagration worsened and worsened.

None of these people around had intentionally hurt me. I didn't want to hurt any of them even though I was ripping them apart with hatred. The fires raged around me from all sides, man and woman alike. I was thinking about all of those who had wronged me in my life. I knew they were lost or trying to get ahead or even just trying to survive. I knew what happened was a type of collateral damage, inflicted on everyone around them because of hatred they felt for themselves. I knew I had people intentionally hurting me, but at some time in their lives they were friends, lovers, and even brothers and sisters. Understanding of this sin came to me in waves.

Even the most angry and hateful of those who violated me were acting out of self-loathing and disgust for themselves. I didn't hate them, or want their destruction. I just hoped they would find themselves and learn what their actions truly stood for.

With the flames of wrath crawling through my spine, I looked deeper into the inferno to see thousands of people who could never let the hatred go. I could tell they blamed others for what happened; they never let go because it was easier to blame.

My legs began to work, so I took a couple steps forward. The flames began to become more intense as those around me, buried under their own hatred, reacted to my movement.

Fire crawled out of me while it danced around me, engulfing me but realizing, deep down, Wrath was never really a part of me. Yes, I'd been to the point of angry stupidity, saying crap I shouldn't have while trying to hurt those in the moment. But it was only ever in that moment. I didn't exact revenge or try to hurt loved ones or business associates.

There is a reason we are supposed to get angry and upset, because when the feeling is kept in your pocket, hateful feelings become wrath, something that can consume your very soul and disrupt your entire life.

The fire that raged from me and through me began to sputter. The fires of Hell didn't consume me anymore. I was vastly surprised at the outcome, and I bypassed several sections of wrath at this time. I saw other tunnels and caves that led to other sections. I turned to look in one. I saw a soul skinning the flesh off of another human being. As I looked closer, it was the same person on both ends.

My soul screamed at this revelation. This soul was tearing himself apart for all eternity. He was both victim and executioner. This being's soul split, and the Id tortured himself.

I saw a flash and could see his prey look like someone else, but it was just a flash, and then it was gone. He was left to mutilate himself while thinking he was acting on revenge. I couldn't see it all. I refused to because it was truly one of the most sickening aspects of cruelty I could ever imagine.

My mind was listening to my own thoughts when it suddenly went blank. I stood there as my vision slowly shrank from the fires of Hell and into darkness. The only thing I had left was a feeling that quickly disappeared as well.

I've walked in the darkness before, hoping to go where I knew I should. But this was different. Every step I took turned me around as if I was walking in a three-foot-wide circle. It spiraled into itself and even though I felt I was walking on a straight path, it just led me into a deeper vortex, spinning me around and around. Where I would stop, nobody knew.

I couldn't see, couldn't taste, touch, smell or hear. But I followed it towards the bottom. I could say I didn't feel, but that would be a mistruth; I could feel I was going downwards. It felt like the changing pressure on an airplane, when you have to swallow to pop your ears. The darkness drank me, only allowing me to move into it. I panicked as my mind clutched onto one thought:

I was on my way towards Pride. I always had an aversion to it. I've always tried to keep myself in check because of it. I've often been lost in the sin of Pride and struggled with it. I knew it was the most seductive of the sins and the most hideous.

I took several small steps, finding a flat surface. I was no longer going down. I took ten more strides and then another ten steps. I knew I was where I was supposed to be. I closed my eyes because this little act became my saving grace. I left the Pit of Wrath and took another step across the next threshold. Everything about me trembled, and my heart—what was left of it—palpitated. My brain felt as if it was convulsing slightly while the blood in my veins froze.

I stopped and apologized to God as if I didn't know what was really going on, even though, in the back of my mind, I did. I felt I was in the worst place imaginable. Getting out of it would be an unimaginable nightmare.

I refused to open my eyes. I couldn't believe where I was. Sure, I've never been lost in my pride; I knew anything I could do, someone could do better. But I saw the fits of pride from my life and knew I was stupid about it. I knew I had been stubborn, egotistical and full myself, letting these actions harm me. I didn't see how it had harmed anyone else, but I guess I was about to.

I realized I was on the last level of Hell that I understood. I've seen a lot of things down here that would turn a man's hair grey. I saw many other tunnels that led to places my mind couldn't completely fathom, so I only saw them faintly.

I tried to open my eyes, but they wouldn't obey. I struggled and even grabbed my eyelids, trying to pry them open. After a minute, my eyelids began to part ever so slowly, allowing me to see just a fraction of what was out there. They stayed that way, partially obscuring what I was trying to discern.

I stopped and let my eyes close again. I tried to make my heart gain a natural rhythm. I willed for everything to stop. I was crazy with fear. I tried harder to stop everything, to stop time and fear. And then something happened.

Time stopped, and everything froze for me. I couldn't feel my heart, and I wasn't breathing. My body died. I felt like the damned. Because I was.

Damned and dead, I opened my eyes, very slowly. I felt a rush. My eyes adjusted while my body began to wither. But it was more than that. Everything I'd felt, thought, judged and experienced folded onto me like a 20-ton weight. It never gave me any release, it just pounded on me. I couldn't shrug it off.

My knees buckled, and I fell to the stone floor. I looked around and found myself lost in a realm of every sin imaginable. I couldn't escape or find solace. I was bare. My mind was naked. I was thrashed on all sides by every single sin and by every single thought and action from my life.

I was at the heart of Hell and I felt I could never escape. I slowly stood up and made my way deeper, to finally find my place, where I belonged. Everything about me began to tighten and convulse as I walked through the last unrepentant doorway.

THE TORTURES OF THE DAMNED AND THE HOPELESSNESS OF PRIDE

A haze of redness whisked all around. It swirled around me like a Cheshire cat, looking for an opening into my being. I tried to scream. It was the worst thing I could have done, because the haze swirled into my mouth and down my throat, ripping my esophagus as it scrambled into my soul. When the redness touched it, my body shook and my blood froze. I panicked and moved my arms, only to feel the ice shatter and rip my veins apart. Still panicking, I fell to my knees, and the ice ruptured everything inside of me. I tried to stand still, but every movement I made tore me apart.

As the torments of Hell began to sink into me, I could feel others all around me. It was still pitch black but I could feel a wave of nausea, as my soul tried to flee but there was no place to go.

A scream came out of nowhere and it burst through me, shattering my insides. The scream became louder and louder, almost cracking my skull. I clutched onto the sides of my head and noticed the scream was coming from me!

As my throat began to burn, the red haze began vomiting out of mouth. I began to force myself to throw up. I dropped to all fours, retching for what seem like an eternity. I felt it puke all out of my system while my veins began to lose their icy consistency. I retched and heaved until I felt empty.

Then a blue haze surrounded me. It too forced its way into my body, through every last opening. This time, I was on fire, and it tore through me like liquid lava.

I fell to a prone position on the floor in agony. Every cell in my body burst into flames. I screamed and rolled around in my own blood, covering myself in gore. The blood began to evaporate from the heat—heat that opened wounds on my body in one instant, then sealing them in the next.

I cried out to God to make it stop!

I cried and cried, knowing I was stuck in Hell and this was just another preliminary. I begged and pleaded when, out of mercy, it was suddenly over.

I lay there and just screamed. And that's when I saw them. That's when they came into my view. My heart broke into a million pieces.

More souls. I crawled to the closest one I could see. I begged for help, but my plea fell on deaf ears.

The person slowly came into focus and I could see it was a woman, a naked woman. She was on top of a pedestal, masturbating in front of a mirror. She was surrounded by others, who were watching, telling her how good and powerful she was.

I called out to her, "Please help me, oh God, please help me!"

She turned from staring at her mirrored image, but she never stopped. Her fingers twirled inside her while the beings around her applauded. I reached her pedestal and began to pull myself up when I was suddenly kicked in the ribs by one of the surrounding beings. I fell back but tried to regain my balance. The woman on the pedestal looked down on me and said, "I am god, and I won't help you."

I began to rise up, trying to get my bearings, when I was kicked again. I rolled away, because I couldn't regain my footing. The woman on the pedestal moaned. One of the figures (the one that had been kicking me) moved closer to her, telling her how powerful and wonderful she was. My eyes were watering, but I could still see hazily. I fixated on the beings around her and began to stare into them. I finally realized that, in each of the surrounding figures, I was witnessing a different characteristic of the woman on the pedestal; they worshipped her with aspects of her own ego.

They were all her. Every last one of them, surrounding herself with love and pride.

My mind shuddered at the implications. I then looked beyond, to the next gathering of people. I crawled towards them. This time, it was a man in a business suit. Standing on an even bigger pedestal, with even more figures around him. He was telling them the secrets to success.

He said, "I know you all came here today to learn how I got rich. I will tell you all this, and more, because I found the secret to life, and it's about listening to me. It's about doing what I say."

Everyone began to applaud and cheer around him, but it was all with the same voice; it was all the same person.

He surrounded himself, worshipping himself by the hundreds. My vision began to improve, opening up my view to see hundreds and thousands of people, all surrounding themselves—with themselves. I saw all the people talking to themselves, in front of thousands of their copies, lying to themselves about prosperity and fame and fortune.

I stumbled forward and hit a mirror, shattering it. The shards dropped everywhere, and I saw another man, staring at himself. When the shards scraped against the floor, they then began to move backwards into what the mirror once was. Whole again, the mirror now blocked my view of the men, so I walked around.

Five naked men, all the same, had the same amount of coins in front of them. They were all in a circle, and there was one dead body lying in the middle. Their eyes darted back and forth, staring at each other. They glanced at their coins and then back again. I couldn't fully understand what was going on until one of them suddenly had a necklace in his hand.

This infuriated the man next to him. A knife materialized in his hand, and he stabbed the man in the neck while yanking the necklace away. The man clutched his neck, falling over, landing on the dead body in the middle. Another knife materialized in the next man's hand, and he stabbed the man with the necklace, so he fell over, dead. He grabbed the necklace, and the pattern repeated as each man stabbed the other to death for the necklace. Like a row of murderous dominoes only found in Hell.

The last man, covered in blood rejoiced over his greed and murder. He lifted the gold necklace high above his head and began to laugh.

The pile of bodies crawled up into itself and regenerated into the men. The newly formed flesh of the men reached out and grabbed the one clutching the knife and necklace, ripping the jewelry away from him. They broke his neck and his body fell to the floor.

Coins began to move as the weight of the Hellborn was shifted. One dead corpse lay in the middle of the men. All of them now had a necklace in their piles.

I stood there, amazed. The five men of the circle were all happy for the revenge and for their greed, but it didn't last long; their eyes began to dart around at each other's piles.

I stepped away. My mind reeled at this never-ending orgy of envy and wrath fueled by pride. I realized he was proud of his envy to the point of murder, and it was wrapped up in greed and wrath on top of it; he was willing to kill himself and every aspect of himself to make it happen.

I fell back down to my knees, begging God to make it stop as my mind began to make the connections. I looked over at the businessman again, giving another speech to himself on how important and wonderful he was. He still went on about riches and finding your dream, saying only he had the answer. He agreed with himself wholeheartedly in front of hundreds of aspects of himself.

He was so proud of his greed that he was on a pedestal, envying himself. His envy and greed was so overpowering that his pride took over and his pride made those sins even stronger.

I began to feel dizzy but was afraid to fall down and find myself stuck in this place. I could barely walk because my mind was staggered by the multi-level complexity of the sins. I walked back to the masturbating woman and saw her more clearly too.

She took pride in her own vanity with lust and surrounded herself with envy; otherwise she wouldn't be watching herself longingly. I walked around her and I suddenly became lost in a sea of souls, somehow prideful of their own sin.

I found myself at the bottom of a mountain of food. On top was a morbidly obese man, surrounded by mirrors. He stared at himself, gorging on the food and relishing it. Each bite was watched slowly as he chewed. The smell of the rotten food began to overpower me. I suddenly realized I could feel again, but I wished I couldn't. I walked around the mountain of decaying fodder when I saw another one. But this mountain was topped by a man surrounded by himself at various weights. No mirrors this time. He was lying on a couch, feeding himself, making the others watch. Each bite he took caused the others to moan in want.

Was the first obese man proud of his vanity and gluttony? Was the second proud of his laziness and even prouder of making them envious of himself? Was it all wrapped around pride and his greediness for food?

I continued to make my way, trying not to get lost, but I surely was. I came upon a woman killing a male version of herself, laughing each time she struck him with an axe. Each blow took a hunk out of her male counterpart. While she was lost in laughter, a replacement of her male self emerged. She hacked into him again, and it repeated. Blood spattered across my face, but I had to watch. I couldn't turn away. Then the next man re-formed and transmogrified into her, and in turn, she turned into him. She had the axe again and lifted it over her head and let it swing deep into what used to be herself.

Then it repeated: The woman killed the male version of herself five times, her anger and wrath wrapped up in pride. Each time, she got to kill the person she felt deserved it, and it was her—albeit the male aspect of herself—and she hated herself for it.

I walked though crowds of people. Thousands of people would surround just one person, themselves. Their sins were supercharged by the sin of pride. Each sin a stumbling block for each soul until pride stepped in, taking over the sin and emblazoning it in the confines of Hell.

I didn't know where I was even though I knew exactly where I was. I began to feel faint as dizziness washed over me. I could still taste the blood on my lips. My ears could only hear the echoes of self-serving people that were talking to themselves while relishing the sins of their lives, and now their sins in Hell. I could feel my heart beat faster as I tried to breathe. But I felt pressure from all around me. My vision spun, and I prayed to God for mercy. I was sorry for living my life the way I had.

Darkness overcame me.

ESCAPE…UNDERSTANDING AND BELIEF: HOPE AND FEAR

I jumped out of bed, about to scream. My body spasmed to the point of unconscious pain. I fell to the floor. Heaving and gasping in total agony, my mind raced to eternity and back within seconds. I jumped up and threw on my clothes.

I knew what I had to do. I ran to the door, grabbing my keys off the coffee table. I stepped out into wonderment.

How can I explain this? The overbearing gorgeousness of reality and of life I took for granted for so long was still there. The windswept forest and blades of grass before my eyes were ever so green that I stopped in mid-stride to breathe the lushness in. Every nuance and every inch and microcosm in every detail swept me away with a beauty I had never known before. Even the cement looked wondrous in its grey manmade pattern. And as for the living things, my eyes almost rolled back into my head for the sheer joy of seeing them again.

That's when dread hit me.

I ran to my car because I knew what was wrong in my heart. It had first come to my attention while going through the Ten Commandments, while God was showing me the way. It was the Second Commandment, and I hadn't even realized it; I hadn't even thought of it as a sin.

My mind kept repeating: "You shall not make for yourself an idol, whether in the form of anything that is in heaven above, or that is in the earth beneath, or that is in the water under the earth."

My mind raced as I opened my car door and jumped in. I pulled out like a madman, starting to feel better, knowing I was going to take care of it. Internally, all I could think about were the life-size rubber corpse and the five-foot rubber alien I had hanging on the wall of my video store. I didn't make these things and wondered if I was crazy for thinking such a thing.

On a conscious level, it was just art. On a subconscious level, I was breaking the 2nd Commandment without even realizing it. I had to take them down as fast as I could.

I pulled out onto the highway, and life was still ten times brighter than I had ever experienced. The sun dazzled my eyes, and the colors leapt out at me. I tried to calm down as I drove.

I thought over and over: "Anything that is in heaven above, or that is in the earth beneath…"

I had a representation of an alien, which is typically above us, and a corpse, which is typically below. I don't know if God actually made aliens someplace else in this galaxy or another. Even angels can be considered aliens, because "alien" means, in the strictest sense, not of this earth.

I swerved and almost slammed into a car in my desperate panic to arrive at my store. It was over 40 minutes away, and I had only been on the road for five. I tried to calm down again when I realized what had happened to me. God visited me. I went to Hell and back. I'd been tempted by demons and Antichrists and false religions and somehow, someway, I'd made it through. I began to think about why God came to me. Why would he choose me over others? I'm not holy. I'm not even a good person. I try, but fail all over the place. I began to think about it, hard. I know I was visited by a demon that tried to manipulate me for months. He tried to turn me away from Christianity. He tried to get me to lose myself in other religions and reincarnation, psychic powers and new-age religion while trying to get me to kill myself. Sending friends and strangers to manipulate me, confuse me, and to stop my search for God. Doing everything It could, to steer me away from the truth. But I held fast. I held onto what He was. I came to a realization at the end, that He was what He was. I couldn't transfer my selective or wishful image of Him onto His actual being. Yet I still marveled at Him. That's when God came, showing me the truth and sending me to Hell to see what it is we really do in our sinful lives.

I laughed because I knew I was saved. I began to feel this wonderment of actually meeting God in the only way I could and I was elated. It is hard to explain how I felt. I was overcome with joy. I yelled out to the Lord, "Thank you God! I knew you would come! I knew you would! Thank you, thank you!"

By this time, I was near my store. Cars zipped by, and the sky was perfectly clear. It was as if I had won the lottery: Your life is safe, no matter what you do. But I had a personal, one-on-one encounter with God, and the feeling was 10,000 times better than any lottery jubilation.

This is when a large convoy of SUVs drove by, over 20 of them at the same time! My mind jumped to the hilarious thought that this was the welcoming committee of a secret Christian society and that they were trying to pull me over to give me the good news. But the cars kept driving past me, and I laughed at myself. Nonetheless, it makes your heart jump when you feel you're part of a family that spreads into eternity. It makes your soul feel safe.

162

I turned onto 22nd Street and drove to my video store. I was anxious to get inside to take the offending things down. Some of you may laugh at this. Others may understand and say, "He's doing what he feels is right."

Still others may say, "He's doing exactly what the Ten Commandments instruct."

I pulled into the parking lot and was inside the store before you can say, "Man on a mission."

I trembled as I walked in. I grabbed my ladder and went to the corpse on my wall. I unscrewed the hooks with my hands, letting it drop like a sack of potatoes onto the floor. It hit with a thud, and I crawled back down the ladder and gave it a nice kick in the ribs. The rubber body made a nice thwack sound. I pulled down the alien, then dragged it to the back room. I let it lie there on the floor.

I felt a lot better. I felt relieved. Really relieved, actually. I picked up the corpse and laid it down in the back as well. I didn't know what I was supposed to do from that point. The sun was shining into my store. I was dazzled by the light when I remembered what day it was. It was Sunday afternoon. I fell to my knees in the store and I began to pray to God. This is how it went:

Dear God,

I thank you for coming to me in my day of need. I thank you for visiting me in my pathetic life I thought that was so important. I know I'm nobody. I know I don't deserve it, and I thank you from the bottom of my soul for showing me the way. I pray you give me the strength and the ability to help others find you. Hopefully, not the way I did, but a lot easier. I want to apologize to you. I didn't realize that you came to me on Sunday morning. To me, it was Saturday night but I'm a night owl and days and nights blend into each other. I have been doing my best not to work on Sundays. My video store is always closed Sunday, which is odd for everyone, but I've been doing it since I opened the place. I would like you to forgive me for working on Sunday. I had to get those offending idols off of my wall because I don't want to offend you so blatantly and be so oblivious as to not respect you. I thank you and pray you forgive me.

Amen.

That's when I fell down and just lay there, laughing to myself. I wondered how I managed to get God to notice me and show me the knowledge I needed.

My life changed for the better after that. I drove back home and picked up the Bible and began reading it from the very beginning. I had never actually read the Bible before. I had read Revelations but that was because of Iron Maiden (I know, shitty reason). This time, it was a totally different story. I ended up quitting drugs, was talked into it only once in a while, and it always ended up like total Hell. I should know.

I did my very best to be a moral, upstanding person. I helped a lot of people, people that needed help or to know the positive side of God. I knew I had one last frontier to conquer, and it was my first love as a child. It was something I had always wanted to do, and that was writing. For years. I studied and read and observed life, religion, philosophy and psychology to find out exactly what had happened to me. At the same time, I learned how to write. I studied the Bible during all this. I was lucky; I had my own company and could work at this sixteen hours a day. I was enthralled by everything I studied and read.

I learned about every religion so I could understand a little more about other people and societies. I learned "nature versus nurture" and the philosophy of Carl Jung and Sigmund Freud. Yes, the concept of the Id and Superego has driven me up the wall ever since. I studied, learned and worked.

One day, walking down the main street of Seventh Avenue in Ybor City, surrounded by thousands of people, I saw a couple of religious people standing in the middle of the street. They talked about Jesus and His forgiveness and about taking hold of Him and letting Him be your Savior.

To digress and catch you up: I had been reading the Bible almost a year at that point. I think—I *think*—I was actually into my second reading of it (I've read it several times now). The one thing I realized from this life and my experiences is that I'm a sinner. I've done my best to stop sinning, but it's impossible. Just thinking about something can be a sin. If you see a commercial with a hot chick or half-naked man in it, you think lustfully and have, in effect, committed adultery of the mind. Same with envy. We see a badass car and say to ourselves, "Oh man! I want that awesomeness!" It is the sin of the covetous.

Matthew 5:22. "He who hates his brother is a murderer!"

If you think about a God other than Him—even if it just feels like a personal belief—God calls it Idolatry. Have you ever used God's name as a curse word? Hitler isn't even a curse word, so if you have, you're a blasphemer! And this is just thoughts, to say nothing of the actual committing of sins as well.

From reading the Bible and personal experience I know we will always commit sin. Thinking you're a good person or even a good Christian means nothing. All of us have fallen short of the Glory of God. That's the meaning of everything.

The Jewish and Christian religions are blood based. Don't ask me why. I've talked to many priests and ministers, and the one question they want to ask God is, "Why blood?"

I've done a lot of soul searching. Doing my best, trying not to sin, but always failing—even after meeting God and going to Hell. The only way I could not sin would be to lie down and not move, think, breath, or interact with anyone, and that's an impossibility. And even then I would be guilty of sloth, so I just can't win! I have a lustful heart. I told you this pages ago, and it still drags on me.

What about the Sabbath? Most of my life, I was taught it was Sunday, but now I hear it is Saturday. Most churches around me are closed on Saturday because they believe that Sunday is the Sabbath. The Jewish people believe Saturday is the Sabbath. I have been working on Saturdays for years and taking Sunday off to honor God. If you live where I live, in a society of fame and greed, then it's an all-out assault against us.

So that's where I had come to in my belief, that day in Ybor City. I needed a sin sacrifice, for the things I did know and for the things I didn't. I needed to come to Jesus and give myself to him. I knew everything I had done and tried to do. I was still confused but was trying with my whole heart. But I found out it was not good enough. I wasn't holier than thou; I'm probably worse than most of you, if not all of you. But I learned to have faith and belief that changed me for the better. I did become a new person. I was nothing like I used to be. I had been reborn and I was about to take the next step.

I walked up to the man preaching to passersby's who wanted nothing to do with his words. I said, "I want to be saved and give myself to Jesus in my heart."

Now he turned to the thousands of people, all strangers walking to and fro, and said, "Here is a man who wants to be saved!"

He laid his hands on me and began praying over me while asking if I would accept this gift in Jesus' name. I don't know exactly the words he spoke, but my eyes were closed and I was amidst thousands of people who didn't care. He prayed and spoke the words and I felt my spirit lift up. Not because of anything mystical but because I believed I was saved and gave my soul to the Lord. Something changed that night; I had a Savior instead of a belief.

My earlier experiences told me God visited, but Jesus had never come up. Jesus became my answer, though I had never met him personally; I had to learn about Him. And I still had to learn from the Bible, even though I had it slapped into my hand and had Hellfire to deal with. It was still left to me to figure out and to grow in faith and belief—as with all of us.

When the street preacher said hallelujah, I smiled brightly and walked away.

It has been years since this happened. I've written movie scripts, getting ready to write this book. Learning everything I can and living life to my best. I've been trying and failing miserably. Just because I found the Lord and danced with the Devil doesn't mean the Devil is not still fighting for me. Quite the contrary. The Devil is probably fighting for me ten times more than before. I do my best but my best is never up to the standards of the Lord, and that's why I have to have a sin sacrifice.

Before we part, I want to tell you what I think actually happened to me.

I know I met something that tried to trick me, sidetrack me and startle me—while using people in my life to cause me to lose hope and make me believe in something false. It did this while masquerading as an Angel and even God. That thing almost had me kill myself. Only then did I give up and just live while still being in awe of the Lord. And that's when He came to me—be it the Lord Himself or an Angel. I was spoken to only through the Bible, the word of God. When the word of the Lord was spoken to me, dread and horror came to me as I learned of my sins and realized I was evil by the words of the Lord.

Ten years ago, I thought I went to Hell. If you ask me today, I might still tell you I did. But after ten years of thinking, analyzing and pondering about where I went, I have other reflections on the matter too. Instead of Hell, maybe the Lord was just showing me what He sees as our sinful nature. Maybe I just saw the sins as they naturally are to the Lord. But then again...

I personally would rather see a Hell made by each and every soul exactly as it wants it. This Hell would be wonderful for the first 10,000 years, but as eternity played out, the agony would likely set in. And yet the creatures I encountered were all lost in themselves, so who knows what they were cognizant of. Maybe the Lord isn't as cruel as we thought. Hellfire and torture, while being eternally raped by demons may just be what we assumed and interpreted.

Each soul has neglected and turned away from the Lord and worshipped his or herself or a desire or object. He gave them what they wanted. He allowed them to turn away from Him and worship and lose themselves in what they wanted most. They will never know the love and kinship of what our Creator has to offer and only in Heaven will that be felt and seen. I like to think, it is Hell enough to have separation from the Lord, even if you have all you think you want and know plenty of self-love. I believe that is the cosmic justice spoken about in the Bible. I believe a loving Lord can give everyone what they think they want and, in doing so, metes out Justice in a way mortals can't conceive.

It's also possible that my "Hell experience" was a way station for those who refuse the Lord. A place for the future damned to wait till the trumpets sound and Revelations begins, for the battle of all men's souls. For those forsook and turned away from the Lord. They may be waiting to be cast into the pit of fire, for their destruction.

I pray that it is death. I pray that the Hell Sermons we hear from so many different Churches, from behind so many pews, are mistaken. I pray that the everlasting fire of the pit is just made for the Devil and those angels who rebelled against the Lord, not for mere mortals who are tricked and manipulated by demons who have studied mankind since the very beginning. They know our weaknesses and they know our souls, even when most of the time we don't even know ourselves in this short life we live.

Ephesians 6:12."For we wrestle not against flesh and blood, but against principalities, against powers, against the rulers of the darkness of this world, against spiritual wickedness in high places."

You might be looking for answers and maybe you received some. I have had the hardest time writing this book, out of worry of being called a false prophet. This weighed on my soul for years, actually, because I was afraid of being judged by the Lord as a false prophet if I spoke to people in His name. I'm also afraid of ministers and clergy and other men of God saying I'm a false prophet. I have never once said, "Here is exactly what the Lord said to me." When I did, it was out of the Holy Bible, which is the word of God. I have, though, told you what the Devil said. I showed you what the Devil did to me in all of his unholy glory. All of His misdirection, manipulation, and traps that I fell into.

Search for God in a safe way. Nothing is safer than opening up a Bible and reading.

I ask and I pray that none of you begin to dabble in the drugs that I explained. I never experienced God while high on LSD and nitrous, only the Devil. Remember that. I implore you to not do what I did. I beg you not to.

I'd like to thank you personally for reading my life's account. It's not your normal Christian book or even a cool drug book that tells you to partake and not worry about the consequences. I know what we all go through in this life. If you know anybody that can understand the places I've been, and you want them to know that even the craziest of us can get a grip—that the worst of us has hope—then give them this book. Pass it on and share. Show others that some of us understand about life and death and, most of all, sin. We can all rise above it and find hope in the only thing that matters: To search for God and never stop looking until He answers you. If you knock on the door long enough, He will answer you. Just be prepared...

Made in the USA
Monee, IL
04 April 2020